RADIO JERUSALEM

local radio reports
some events
in the first century

Charles J Kitchell

GINN and COMPANY Ltd
18 Bedford Row
London WC1R 4EJ

Acknowledgements

The photographs are reproduced by permission of the following:
page 10 Picturepoint Ltd; pages 20, 57, 87 the Bible Lands Society;
pages 30, 67, 77 Brian Bracegirdle; page 40 C.J. Bucher Publishers Ltd, Lucerne and Frankfurt.

The photograph on the cover is of the tower glass by John Piper in
Liverpool Metropolitan Cathedral, and is reproduced by permission
of the Shell International Petroleum Company Ltd.

The designs for the cover and the title page are by Terry Lelliott.

© C.J. Kitchell 1972   107202   ISBN 0 602 21844 6
Published by Ginn and Company Ltd, 18 Bedford Row, London WC1R 4EJ
Printed in Great Britain by Stott Brothers Ltd, Halifax

CONTENTS

<u>PREFACE</u>

These eight scripts were written for the B.B.C., Radio Leeds, as an occasional series of fifteen-minute evening news bulletins, as though Jerusalem had local radio facilities at the time of certain major events in the life and times of Jesus.

As with authentic news programmes, the basic pattern does not vary: station theme music opens and closes the bulletin; a newscaster has general news items, sometimes including a weather forecast, for the beginning and the end; and the middle seven or eight minutes are taken up with the reporting of that day's major event through the interviews and comment by the roving reporter, Jonathan ben Etchel.

Encouraged by the approval of my first script by Phil Sidey, Director of Radio Leeds, though somewhat daunted by experience of the high standard of broadcasting he demanded, I rehearsed actors from among the students and staff of the City of Leeds and Carnegie College, produced the performance, added extra sound effects, and edited the final tape-recordings.

The intention was that listeners in general should hear and feel for themselves the kind of people who played their part in the world into which Jesus came, their response to him, and Jesus himself as he appeared to them and made himself known to them. Jesus himself is never interviewed. It was a pleasant surprise to have fellow-teachers and student-teachers in Leeds asking to be allowed to use these tapes - some preferred the scripts, or both scripts and tapes - in the classroom or morning assembly. I was delighted when it was reported that they had sparked off some fresh appreciation of their subjects with top juniors and various secondary school age groups.

Long a practitioner of the conviction that all subjects in the curriculum can be enlivened and enlightened by elements of drama-tisation, I am grateful to the publishers for this opportunity to offer these little things to a wider teaching and learning public, in the hope that any imaginative skill I have may help others to consider, again or for the first time, the Good News in a modern form.

4

<u>TEACHERS' NOTES</u>

Although these eight scripts were originally written for broadcasting,
it is hoped that in their printed form they will be put to a variety of
uses. In the classroom they can be read either quietly or aloud with
the pupils taking the different parts, or performed with or without
costume. They can be acted either in the classroom or in the hall at
morning assembly to simulate radio or television broadcasts. A whole
class can participate in making a recording of a script for its own
entertainment and for 'broadcasting' to a wider audience.

Classroom exercises

One simple way of using the scripts is for pupils, after a preliminary
reading and rehearsal, to come forward and read their parts in
relevant groups. This can be effective, if care is taken over the
choice of readers. For example, when the recordings were made for
Radio Leeds, we liked to choose a deep fruity voice for the superior
tones of Caiaphas, the High Priest.

Costumes

A costume performance can be organised informally in class, if the
necessary clothes are fairly easy to obtain. Acting in costume is
fun, and perhaps with greater involvement more will be gained by
pupils from the scripts and from the experience generally. When a
performance is given before an audience - perhaps another class,
perhaps a proportion or whole of the rest of the school at morning
assembly - it is a more formal occasion, and the costumes need
careful preparation.

If there are no suitable outfits available in the school, collecting
them together can be an intimidating task. Jumble sales are an
excellent source of material. A teacher normally can also assemble
a considerable amount of material by asking all kinds of people if
they have anything to contribute. Many pupils will enjoy collecting
all manner of things, and if they are enthusiastic, friends and relatives will in many cases be willing and able to help both by giving
away old garments and helping to make new ones.

Making the correct costumes should involve a certain amount of research, perhaps on the part of the pupils as well as the teacher. The following books give examples of Roman and Jewish dress in New Testament times: <u>Ancient Greek, Roman and Byzantine Costume</u> M.G. Houston, A. and C. Black; <u>Costume in Antiquity</u> J. Laver, Thames and Hudson; <u>A History of Jewish Costume</u> A. Rubens, Vallentine Mitchell.

Here also are some suggestions, which are the result of my experience of staging plays of this kind.

<u>Tunics</u>
The tunic, both Jewish and Roman, was worn to the knees by young men, and to the ankles by older men and all women. A large oblong piece of material is needed for either of these. No cutting out is necessary. Fold the cloth in half lengthwise, and cut a slit in the middle of the fold to provide an opening for the head. Allow the garment to hang loosely, and gather it in round the waist with a rope, cord or strip of another cloth. If the tunic is too long, any depth of loosely stitched hem is better than cutting the material short.

Tunics for Jews should be colourful, and made of rough or smooth cloth, according to the character's profession.

<u>Headgear</u>
Jewish women wear squares of cloth on their heads, perhaps in colours which contrast with their tunics. These squares can be tied under the chin like a modern head scarf, or clipped on to the hair and left hanging loosely round the shoulders. Jewish men wear a square or oblong piece of cloth secured by a rope or cord headband. Men and women in Roman dress can wear plain fillets of leather, gold, silver or coloured braid.

<u>Trimmings</u>
The decoration of all costumes should be done in broad striking lines. More delicate decoration is not effective on the stage. A broad band of orange or scarlet, about 30 centimetres wide, round the hem of a coat or cloak is worth more than yards of delicate lace. Fur is a particularly effective trimming, giving weight and dignity. Elderly aunts and grandmothers often can give away old pieces of fur. However, if fur is not available, swansdown is a good, cheap substitute.

<u>Jewellery</u>
Fine jewellery can be made from tin and sheet lead, which can be
gilded. Members of the class can produce with these materials, at
small expense, all the crowns, girdles and necklaces that are required.
Ordinary coarse twine, gilded or silvered, makes effective necklaces
and bracelets if funds are not available to buy cheap chains from a
hardware store. (See <u>Creative Metalcraft</u> Creative Play Series 8,
Batsford; <u>Working with Wire, Wood and Cork</u> Colour Crafts 4,
Macdonald; <u>Homemade Enamel Jewelry</u>, <u>Bead Necklaces</u> Leisure
Crafts Series, Search Press.)

<u>Armour</u>
Real armour is expensive, difficult to obtain and extremely trouble-
some to wear. One of the best ways of getting a convincing effect
of armour is to use the cheapest coarse dish cloths. Stitch them
together as required, and spray or paint them with silver gilt. The
result is magnificent chain mail. Alternatively, a long, grey sweater
coat can be lightly painted or sprayed with silver.

A helmet is easily made from the top of an old felt hat - bowler hats
are ideal for this purpose. Remove the brim, cut the crown to the
appropriate shape, sew or staple on any projections and finish it off
with a coat of glue size and a coat of aluminium powder paint. The
collar of the 'chain mail' sweater can be attached to the rim of the
helmet so that only the face is left exposed. Leggings of any knitted
material, similarly treated, complete the costume.

<u>Television News Bulletin</u>
An effective way of using the scripts in the classroom or for morning
assembly on stage is to produce something which can be called a
television news bulletin. Set to one side of the stage is the newscaster in his 'studio'. This is in a small area separated from the
rest of the stage by a screen. There the newscaster sits behind a
desk with a mock or real microphone in front of him and a large clock
on the wall behind. The rest of the space on the stage is used for
acting the interviews, with the roving reporter moving to the side of
the stage away from the newscaster for his linking pieces. When
the reporter is in the studio with the newscaster, he moves over to
join him on the other side of the screen. Use of the scripts in this
way at morning assembly on the stage in the school hall, can be

made more effective by introducing simple lighting effects, such
as alternating the lighting of the studio and the rest of the stage
according to the script. However, rehearsal of the lighting is as
important as rehearsal of the cast itself, as sloppy or ill-timed
lighting can ruin the whole performance.

An alternative is to put the newscaster offstage, leaving the whole
stage free for acting the interviews.

<u>Radio News Bulletin</u>
For pupils to prepare their own tape recording the basic requirements are:
a) two tape recorders b) one record player c) a reasonably sound-
proof room to be used as the recording studio. A classroom with
closed windows and drawn curtains is usually suitable for this
purpose, while a school hall, which in nearly all cases has an echo,
is not. If desired, the whole class can be organised into a prod-
uction team. This team will include the producer, his assistants,
the casting director and his assistants, the studio manager and his
assistants, the technicians (including an effects unit) and the
actors.

The whole team should first go through the script together to get an
idea of the technical and artistic requirements. Then, while
members of the effects unit are searching out and experimenting
with background noises, the producer should rehearse the cast.
Remember that the dramatised scenes must be acted as in a play.
Clear diction is essential, so also is variety of expression in the
reading. Never rush into the final recording, but always have plenty
of rehearsals. Some of these rehearsals should be recorded and
played back. At this stage, correct working distances from the
microphone for different actors should be determined. The microphone picks up the slightest sound, so no one should move about or
shuffle his feet while recording, and great care should be taken not
to rustle the pages of the script. Unstapled sheets should be slid
quietly under each other.

While the cast is rehearsing the spoken parts, the effects unit
should be selecting appropriate sound effects. Nowadays almost
every conceivable kind of background noise is obtainable from record
libraries. Careful attention should be given to the background

noises for the roving reporter's contributions. If he is in the studio
with the newscaster no background is required, but if he is 'out and
about' his efforts must be made more realistic with sound effects of
noises for crowds, animals, wind and so on.

Throughout these eight 'news bulletins', I found that the only sound
effect that had to be made at the time of recording the speech was
that for the crucifixion party of soldiers playing dice at the foot of
the cross. Two 'extras' held a solid board high near the microphone
into which others were speaking, while a third rolled the dice on
cue. For that particular sequence, thunder was the only other effect
added later from a record.

The final recording can proceed as follows:

a) record all the spoken parts on one tape, preferably all on the
same occasion, but not necessarily in their proper order if this is
difficult to manage. A few seconds of blank tape should be left between each sequence to facilitate adding sound effects and editing.

b) The next stage is to record the speeches and the sound effects
on the second tape recorder. A sound effect should be set up on the
record player, and the speech tape on the first tape recorder. Both
instruments should be arranged so that their loudspeakers point
directly at the microphone of the second tape recorder. Before
embarking on the final recording of each speech, experiment with
levels of sound of the background noise against the speech until the
desired balance is achieved. Often the best result with an episode
is achieved by fading up the sound effect before the speech begins,
and fading down after it ends.

c) The last stage is that of editing the tape, to put the different
sequences into their correct order, and to make any necessary cuts.
Basic tape editing kits are obtainable from most tape suppliers, and
have full instructions. Never use ordinary 'sellotape' for splicing
tape. If your tape recorder is capable of different speeds - $3\frac{3}{4}$ inches
per second is the usual speed - recording at the faster speed of $7\frac{1}{2}$
inches per second makes editing easier and the overall sound fuller.
The process of tape editing can sound difficult and intimidating, but
with practice amateurs can do it easily and successfully.

An Arab village in Galilee

Evening News Bulletin I

<u>THE NATIVITY</u>

Newscaster

Reporter, Jonathan ben Etchel

Shepherd, Michael

Innkeeper, Issachar ben Cleophas

Zealot

Jewish Woman

Roman Lawyer, Curtius Nerva

Joseph

Mary

(Fade in station music ....)

NEWSCASTER   This is Radio Jerusalem. Before the news - in which we
hear from our own reporter of some sensational happenings in Bethlehem - here is the weather forecast:
for the Coastal Plain and Central Highlands - a cloudy
day is expected throughout the region tomorrow, with the
likelihood of heavy showers later.
Temperature, about the seasonal average - 10°C.
Outlook - continuing wet.
And for the Jordan Valley - a bright, crisp day after
another clear, starry night; mostly sunny, with
occasional light cloud.
Temperature, cool - around 7°C.
Outlook - continuing fine.
Now some of today's headlines: Antipater, Herod the
Great's eldest son, is planning to leave Rome soon. He
hopes to be back in Caesarea in a few weeks time.
15,000 tonnes of Egyptian corn have been distributed
either free or at rock-bottom prices to the people of Rome.

11

300,000 folk have each received fifty kilograms of corn from the Emperor Augustus as part of this year's 'grain dole'.
For today's big news we go over to Bethlehem with its 'heavenly choir' sensation, and a newborn baby found in a pub backyard. This sensational news comes as a climax to the past few days of census-taking, in which thousands from all over the country have been converging on their family homes to register both themselves and their families. Jonathan ben Etchel reports:

(Fade in outside effect - no specific noises)

REPORTER Here in Bethlehem excitement is focussed on some local shepherds who report seeing an angel on the hillside outside the town! Not content with that, they claim to have heard what they call "the heavenly choir"! At about noon today I spoke to one of these shepherds:

(Fade up background of people and sheep)

Michael, tell me, what _did_ happen last night?

MICHAEL We were out in the fields. We're generally out there all night keeping an eye on the sheep. Usually it's a quiet job. But last night, suddenly, there was a brilliant light, and before we had time to say anything about it, a voice started speaking to us.
Imagine how we felt. I know I was scared stiff - I'm sure the others were too. None of us is the sort of fellow who goes in for ghosts - but - well, that was no ordinary man last night. The light was too bright to see clearly, but I reckon it was one of God's angels! Now I don't reckon to be a coward, but I don't mind admitting I was all set to get away from that spot, and quick.

REPORTER Can you remember what this - er - being - said?

MICHAEL Could I ever forget it! "Don't be afraid," it said, "I've got good news for you! The Messiah has been born in Bethlehem today. If you want proof, you'll find a baby lying in a manger." Immediately there was the sound of the loudest singing I've ever heard, coming from a great choir of creatures, gleaming like fire, where the angel had stood.

REPORTER   Could you make out what they were saying?

MICHAEL   Very clearly. It was: "Glory to God in the highest heights and on earth peace to the men whose welfare he ever seeks."

 (Pause)

REPORTER   I see! Then what?

MICHAEL   Eh? Oh yes, well, everything was back to normal. It was pitch dark again. For a moment or two it was a bit tricky. I mean, I began to wonder if I'd gone funny. I couldn't make up my mind whether to speak to the others about it or not. But when young Benjamin - he's only a kid really - blurted out, "What was all that?" I suppose we all realised. We'd all seen it, and heard it.

REPORTER   So what did you do?

MICHAEL   We set off for the town. I think we were all glad to get away from that spot anyhow. It was behind the pub, in the stables that we found a baby lying on the straw in the manger.

 (Pause)

REPORTER   What, just a baby, lying there on its own?

MICHAEL   Oh no, the mother was there - just a young girl really - she was resting. Her husband was pottering around, tidying up, I think. We told them what had happened to us.

REPORTER   That must have shocked them!

MICHAEL   Now that's another strange thing, it didn't seem to surprise them at all. In fact, the way she smiled at us I'd swear she'd known about it all along.

 (Fade out sound effects)

<u>The Nativity</u>

REPORTER   Some story, you'll agree! And I decided to check on it
              with the local innkeeper. Eventually, I got him in a
              corner on his own, in his pub:

                  (Fade in pub noises, with occasional
                  sheep's bleat)

              Issachar ben Cleophas - what's the real story of someone
              using your stable last night?

ISSACHAR   Well, you know what it's been like here - hoards of folk
              passing in for this census thing. Good for business, I
              can tell you, wish I'd had ten times more rooms in my
              pub. This man and woman arrived after dusk, asking for
              a room for the night. It was ridiculous, every room's
              been taken for days. "But my wife's pregnant - any time
              now," he said. What can you do? In the end I offered
              them the use of the stable out back. I mean, at least
              they could be dry and warm. I left them to settle in as
              well as they could. I was too busy in the pub, as you
              can see.

REPORTER   Did you see anything of them during the night, or later?

ISSACHAR   All I know is that I was disturbed at some ungodly hour
              by a rumpus outside. The noise was coming from the
              back. When I went out there were some shepherds bab-
              bling away. Michael was among them, normally quite a
              sensible chap. They were pouring out some story about
              angels and the birth of the Messiah!

REPORTER   And what do <u>you</u> think?

ISSACHAR   Eh?

REPORTER   What do you think of it all?

ISSACHAR   Me? Well, for heaven's sake! I mean in my back-yard?

REPORTER   Quite! Can I see the couple in your stable?

ISSACHAR   'Fraid not, they've already gone. Didn't say where to.
              Just as well, if you ask me - no good can come from that
              sort of thing.

<u>The Nativity</u>

(During last two sentences a rising voice heard
through general background chatter, and now it is
heard haranguing the crowd with ...)

ZEALOT   Who needs a Messiah anyhow? I've had my fill of them.
Freedom is what we want, and we've got to go out there
and take it - ourselves.

REPORTER   You, sir, why are you so worked up about all this?

ZEALOT   I'm a Zealot - and I don't care who knows it! A Messiah?
Look, we've been talking about a Messiah - huh! - even
praying for one for ages, and where's it got us? The
jackboot of Rome on our necks, Herod and his lot on our
backs! What I say is, we've got to up and fight, and ...

REPORTER   Yes, yes - but what about this baby?

ZEALOT   Baby? What's special about a baby? Look, chum, this
is a man's world. Whoever heard of a manger as a
throne? Forget it man.

WOMAN'S
VOICE   What do you mean, "A man's world?" (audibly spits)

REPORTER   So what do you make of it, ma'am?

WOMAN   A new baby is always good excuse for celebrating, and
specially when it's a boy. Let's have a real party! And,
of course, we must thank God for it. My, that was a
fine wee lad born out there last night. Don't you pay
much attention to this lot, sir, most of the time they
don't know what they're on about.

(Raising her voice above crowd)

You lot, say what you like! I'm telling you, that baby
might be a great one some day - so there!

(Fade out pub noise)

REPORTER   It is well known that among the Jews the party that has
worked harder than any other over the years to maintain
speculation about angels and the flowering of the hoped-
for Messiah, is that of the Pharisees. But none of their

leaders was available for official comment when I sought
them out to face them with last night's happenings.
However, off-the-record as it were, one Pharisee did
concede that ever since the brilliant reign of King David
the conviction had grown that from his line there would
come, eventually, one greater than he who would estab-
lish what he called, "the kingdom": this one would be a
deliverer, in fact, the Messiah.
When I quoted the Zealot's outburst to him, the Pharisee
was pretty heated himself in his condemnation of any
suggestion of revolution or uprising. "In God's good
time," was the phrase he preferred, "a son of David
would appear to fulfil the Law."
As I questioned him further about the promised Messiah,
he did admit, somewhat reluctantly, I thought, that about
700 years ago a prophet, Micah, had preached such a
one to be born in Bethlehem. But he was quick to counter
any link with today's Bethlehem story as he scornfully
pointed me to the shepherd messengers: "Didn't I know
that shepherds were despised as quite unable to keep the
ceremonial law? Why, they couldn't even observe all
the special hand-washings, let alone the more compli-
cated rules and regulations - and God could hardly be
expected to have dealings with such common people."
So much for the Pharisees' position!
The one Sadducee I found at home retorted with an em-
phatic "No comment." But then they don't believe in
angels anyway!
As I moved around the town, with some difficulty in these
great crowds, I came across the usual small groups of
Roman soldiers, occupied with their seemingly never-
ending games of dice. Even as they gamed their time
away, there was some talk of the night's disturbances,
mainly, I noticed, among the new recruits from Rome,
as they asked about angels and messiahs, and the like.
I couldn't help but remark how the old-hands were
wanting to cut them short with warnings of "treason".
"It was only some country bumpkins - potty, I expect"
was one remark I overheard. Another was, "King Herod

may be a sick old man but he's still the boss-man here,
and don't you forget it."
After lunch I joined other reporters outside the Palace of
Herod, just in time for the latest bulletin by his medical
advisers being posted on the main gate. I quote:
>   "The health of King Herod the Great still gives
>   cause for concern: his condition is critical
>   following another slight heart attack this morning
>   after a very unsettled night." Unquote.
This statement was timed as at noon today.
Palace spokesmen refused to comment on the suggestion
that the King's relapse was in any way connected with
these latest rumours of a Jewish Messiah.
Later this afternoon I visited the house of Curtius Nerva,
the well-known Roman lawyer. I told him the story and
asked if he had any opinions on it.

(Fade in large room effect)

CURTIUS   Oh, no! Not another one. Have you ever been to
            Hermontis?

REPORTER   No.

CURTIUS   It's worth a trip. There's a fresco there in a temple - a
            kneeling mother and a wondrous child, surrounded by
            heavenly creatures. And those goddesses really are
            something - yes! - the whole thing is bathed in the light
            of a fair sunrise! Do you know who the mother and child
            are? Cleopatra and her son Ptolemy Caesar!

REPORTER   Ye gods!

CURTIUS   You want my opinion? I can't see a birth in some country
            pub back premises rating very high alongside Cleopatra
            and her child, can you? In fact, if this story of yours
            gets around that Bethlehem couple and their brat could be
            in real trouble.

(End of large room effect)

REPORTER   And on that cautionary note, back to the Jerusalem
            studio.

NEWSCASTER — Thank you, Jonathan ben Etchel - who sent us that report over the wire just an hour ago.
And that's all for this news bulletin. With a reminder that our microphones will be covering Sunday's demonstration. Yes, we'll be there when the demonstrators march on the Temple in protest against the golden eagle that King Herod has set up over the great door.
Our main news is at the usual hour of ....

(Interruption. Studio telephone rings, newscaster excuses himself, picks it up, curt "Yes", and ...)

(pause) I see - can you put him on direct? Good. We have Jonathan ben Etchel through to us again on a direct line with some on the spot news from Bethlehem.

(Following speeches from Jonathan sounding like long distance telephone call, with running water sound in background)

REPORTER — I'm on the road out north from Bethlehem which leads to Bethany, and I've just caught up with the controversial couple and their baby. They're resting by a stream. Joseph, isn't it?

JOSEPH — Yes, that's right.

REPORTER — All this fuss about your baby son born last night .... what do you make of it?

JOSEPH — Really, I don't know. I can tell you I was worried for my wife's safety at times. It was bad enough not being able to find shelter last night. Nobody seemed to want to know! But this morning's rumpus - all that talk about the Messiah! I just don't know.

REPORTER — Can't you think of any explanation at all?

JOSEPH — Well, I am of David's line, but you can see for yourself. Hardly royal, are we? I mean, I'm only a carpenter, and the wife, Mary, is no one special.

REPORTER — Even so, you must have some ....

The Nativity

MARY   (Interrupts quietly but firmly with . . . .)
                My heart is full of the greatness of God,
                my spirit thrills to God my Saviour.
                He has looked kindly upon me, as humble as I am,
                and I am blessed above all imagining.
                From now on, everyone will call me blessed!

                (Silence except for running stream.
                Sound of telephone line disconnected . . .)

NEWSCASTER   Er – well – er – we apologise for the poor reception on
             that line. And that seems to be all from Bethlehem. Our
             main news will be at the usual hour – 11 o'clock. Until
             then,
                        good evening!

                     (Station music
                      and fade out)

The wilderness of Jordan

Evening News Bulletin II

THE BEHEADING OF JOHN

Newscaster

Reporter, Jonathan ben Etchel

Herod's Chamberlain

Zealot

Jewish Woman

Nicodemus, Elder of the Sanhedrin

John the Baptist

Levite

(Fade in station music ....)

NEWSCASTER
This is Radio Jerusalem.
John the Baptiser is dead.
He was beheaded by order of Herod Antipas in the early hours of this morning at the climax of an all-night party given at the castle of Machaerus to honour the thirtieth anniversary of the Tetrarch's accession.
After dancing before the guests, Salome, the daughter of Herod's new wife Herodias, was offered anything she cared to ask by the Tetrarch. After a brief consultation with her mother, she asked for the prophet's head to be served on a silver dish.
The news of this dramatic and bloodthirsty request is spreading like wildfire through the Jordan Valley.
Jonathan ben Etchel reports:

(Fade in sinister wind effects)

REPORTER
The castle of Machaerus: standing on a lonely ridge, surrounded by terrible ravines, and overlooking the east side of the Dead Sea - surely one of the loneliest,

21

grimmest and most unassailable fortresses in the world.
Certainly that's how it looked to me this afternoon, as I
watched a group of grown men, weeping as they stumbled
down the stony track, carrying away the prophet's
remains to be prepared for a decent burial.
Anger and sorrow were mingled in their mourning - anger
at what they and thousands of others are calling cold-
blooded murder, sorrow at the loss of their beloved John.
In the less bleak living quarters of the castle I spoke to
the Tetrarch's Chamberlain. I asked him to describe for
us the events leading up to the party's shocking end.
Somewhat warily, he told me this story:

    (Fade out wind,
    fade in background palace music)

CHAMBERLAIN The party was given to celebrate the thirtieth anniversary
of His Highness's confirmation as Tetrarch of Galilee and
Peraea by Augustus Caesar. A large number of local
officials, including leading figures in both civil and
military authorities, were present at the dinner, and at
the entertainment which followed.
Of course the wine on these occasions is apt to flow
freely, and in the early hours of the morning the gentlemen were beginning to grow a little restive, until Miss
Salome, His Highness's step-daughter, danced
before him.

REPORTER   What sort of dance was this?

CHAMBERLAIN Er - perhaps it _was_ a somewhat improper dance for a
young lady of her station. But it clearly pleased the
gentlemen, judging by their long and loud applause. And
His Highness was most impressed too. Perhaps a little
rashly he cried out that the young lady could have anything she cared to name, up to half his tetrarchy!

REPORTER   Please go on.

CHAMBERLAIN Well, after a pause, while she left the room (apparently
to consult with her mother) she returned and asked
for the prisoner John's head, upon a silver dish. His

Highness was visibly upset at the request - but he <u>had</u> promised, and no doubt felt he couldn't go back on <u>that</u>. Reluctantly, he ordered the execution to take place.

REPORTER	Then what?

CHAMBERLAIN	A few minutes later one of the soldiers appeared with the grisly object, on a silver dish. It was presented to Miss Salome. She - er - took it to her mother. (boldly) I feel sure I can say that His Highness regards the incident as most unfortunate.

		(Fade out palace music, fade in wind)

REPORTER	On the streets there seemed to be no other topic of conversation but this morning's execution! Everyone was bursting with something to say on the subject:

		(Fade out wind, fade in noisy street sounds - much chatter)

ZEALOT	Cold-blooded murder, that's what it is!

WOMAN	Things have come to a pretty pass when a tetrarch humours the whim of a slip of a girl by cutting off a prisoner's head to add spice to the excitement of a drunken party. <u>Men</u>!! huh!

ZEALOT	You can picture the merry scene at Machaerus, can't you! Stuffed with rich foods and inflamed with fine wines. Herod and his party revelling noisily in the entertainment; and all the while, deep down in dungeons, a man of God, a prophet, a latter-day Elijah, lies chained - waiting and wondering what that far-off row can mean. Oh! I can see it all - the dancing reaching its climax with the night's unexpected star turn; Salome, Herodias' daughter - flushed with excitement at the success of her display; then those fateful words, from the Tetrarch himself: "Say what you want, anything, just ask!" - Makes you want to throw up!

WOMAN	Mind you, I don't blame that lass Salome - well, not altogether. Perhaps she's not all she should be, but she's just a pawn in the hands of that vicious, revengeful woman, used as a tempter for a drunken princeling. And <u>he</u> falls head-first into the trap, too proud, or too scared to go back on his stupid oath.

ZEALOT   So what? The prophet John is dead! And thousands mourn him, <u>and</u> wait for divine judgment to strike down his murderers. This vile act will go down in history, you mark my words it will.   (raising voice threateningly) Be warned, Tetrarch, you've dug your own grave!

(Fade out street noises, fade in wind again)

REPORTER   In the absence of the High Priest I went to the home of that revered elder statesman of the Sanhedrin, Nicodemus, to ask for his recollections of last night's victim. True to his reputation, I found him in his garden surrounded with playful children:

(Fade out wind, fade in sounds of children outdoors)

NICODEMUS   (laughingly)   Now, now, children, run along and play over there for a while. <u>You too</u>, Deborah! Now, young man. Ah, yes, John. Terrible business! I remember his father well. One of the old school, he was. Never could understand why he insisted on living out there in the hill country. Good old Zechariah! Mind you, he never neglected his Temple duties.

REPORTER   Quite. What about his son, John?

NICODEMUS   Eh? ah! Young John. What a boy – bit of a rip, he was. Wasn't a bit surprised when he grew up the way he did. Stirred folk up, eh? For all his unusual habits, look what he's done. Thousands of people going to him to be baptised in the Jordan. Who'd have thought it?

REPORTER   You remember his childhood, then?

NICODEMUS   Mmm ... respectable parents, and orthodox, I'm sure – never paid much attention myself to rumours of goings-on in some of those hill villages. Zechariah, his father,

was a priest of the Abijah family, and his mother,
Elizabeth, traced her ancestry from one of the old
princely families. Both been dead for many years now.
At least they've been spared today's shocking affair.

REPORTER   Yes, indeed.

NICODEMUS   There were some unusual stories, I can tell you, around
             the hill villages about the birth of John. They'll be
             trotting them all out again now. I remember well the
             widespread surprise - and delight - which greeted the
             news that Zechariah and Elizabeth were expecting a
             child.   It had long been assumed they'd never have
             a family.

REPORTER   Wasn't there some talk of an angel visitation?

NICODEMUS   So you've heard about that. Yes, I suppose you radio
             men would. Zechariah did claim that the Angel Gabriel
             appeared to him one day in the Temple sanctuary.
             Promised him a son who would one day be a prophet.
             Certainly that was the time when Zechariah lost his voice
             suddenly. Never spoke again until the day of his son's
             circumcision. Almost a whole year he was dumb. Angel
             or no angel, that boy was no mean prophet.

             (Fade out children, fade in wind)

REPORTER   A fiery preacher, John could always be relied upon to
             attack abuses in contemporary society. As we have
             reported from time to time, he included both Pharisees
             and Sadducees in his zealous criticisms of present-day
             religion and behaviour. He was no respecter of persons -
             in one sermon I heard, he called them "snakes"; on
             another occasion he likened them to trees which had
             failed to bear any fruit, fit only to be chopped down and
             burned. Again and again he warned them <u>not</u> to rely on
             their religious ancestry, not to feel virtuous because
             Abraham was their forefather!
             This brand of straight talking wasn't exactly calculated
             to win friends for John, and no one was surprised, I
             imagine, when that powerful deputation of Priests and

Levites tackled him some time ago. You may remember
that one of the Levite members had this to say at
the time:

> (Fade out wind, fade in sounds of crowd chatter
> and running water.   John preaching through
> it all)

JOHN   Repent! I tell you, repent!
You offspring of vipers! Who warned you to flee from the
wrath to come?
Repent, and be baptised with water, for one stronger
than I is coming.

> (Begin to fade out John)

I'm not fit to stoop down to untie the strap of his
sandals - the one who will baptise you with the Holy
Spirit, with fire! Repent! Repent!

> (Fade to background effect only)

LEVITE   Just look at him! Could anything be more obvious? The
man's mad, he's a wild animal!

REPORTER   Did your deputation have any success with him?

LEVITE   We come here in the name of no less an authority than
the High Priest himself, but does <u>he</u> care? Yet he's
clever in his madness. Wasn't going to be tricked when
we asked him, "Who are you? Are you the Messiah?"
Cunningly evasive he was when he said he wasn't
Messiah, but simply a voice crying in the desert.

REPORTER   - But crying what? what <u>is</u> his message?

LEVITE   He goes on about "making the Lord's Highway straight"!
"Prepare the way!" he screams at them.

REPORTER   I don't understand. The way for whom?

LEVITE   You might well ask. He doesn't even claim to be one of
the promised prophets expected to precede the coming of
Messiah. We asked him straight out, "Then why are you
baptising all these people?"   Said his baptism is only

a symbolic cleansing in water, and that there's to be
baptism with the Spirit and with fire to follow, but not
by him.

REPORTER   That's what I'm not clear about. Who?

LEVITE   All I can tell you is what he himself said. See what you
can make of it. He claimed that the one who would fulfil
all this is actually standing in that crowd - right there in
that lot - but unrecognised by priests and people alike.
(heatedly)   Look at 'em - one of <u>them</u>? Beats me what
they see in him.

(Fade out, fade in wind again)

REPORTER   Mad or not, an impressive figure of a man was John. He
made his mark, and not least because of his courage. It
was quite clear to all who heard him that he would prefer
death to falsehood. I suppose it was inevitable that
even the Tetrarch would come under the lash of his
tongue, accused of outraging the laws of decency and
morality in his second marriage.
And it has to be conceded that seldom in history can
there have been such complex matrimonial entanglements
as exist in the Herod family - and the latest is no
exception. As a direct result of the Tetrarch's visit to
Rome, Heriodias, the wife of his half-brother Philip, left
her husband to marry him. So Herodias is at once his
wife, his sister-in-law, and his niece as the daughter of
another half-brother, Aristobulus! At the very least the
Tetrarch has broken Jewish law by such a marriage. This,
and more, that child of the desert and of the wide open
spaces, John the Baptiser denounced - and died today.
But the questions will go on! Why did a teenaged girl
ask for such a gruesome present? Why did Herodias
allow her young daughter to perform what the Chamberlain
primly called "a somewhat improper dance" in the early
hours at a stag party? How could the Tetrarch make such
a rash oath? And follow it through to such an end? The
manner of John's death demands answers to these
questions.

<u>The Beheading of John</u>

(Fade out wind)

NEWSCASTER   Now for the rest of the news.
The Zealot party is steadily growing in numbers again. Throughout Judaea small groups of uncompromising men are reported to be awaiting their chance to attempt a coup d'état. A Roman spokesman dismissed them as being (I quote) "a minute band of undesirables whose activities are under observation".

It is reported that a local plasterer has been miraculously healed in Capernaum synagogue by Jesus of Nazareth. Yesterday he went as usual to worship, nursing his paralysed right arm. During the service a controversy arose over whether or not it was legal for acts of healing to take place on the Sabbath, and, according to our eye-witness's account, Jesus took the man's arm, and restored it to normal – despite the vocal and angry opposition of a group of Pharisees.

For the second time since he became procurator, Pontius Pilate is at loggerheads with Jewish leaders over alleged sacrilege. The cause of the present crisis is his recent action in hanging a number of gilded shields on the interior walls of the procuratorial place here in Jerusalem. Sanhedrin officials have registered a complaint against what they describe as "blatant sacrilege". They maintain that the shields contravene the law against graven images in exactly the same way as the regimental standards did in the previous controversy. Pilate met a deputation this morning, consisting of the chief magistrates of the Sanhedrin who attempted to convey to him the grave concern which is being widely expressed among Jewish people at what they regard as deliberate provocation by the Procurator. The Governor is said to have made it clear that he cannot in any sense regard the shields as idolatrous since they consist simply of gilded metal, decorated only with the words "Tiberias Caesar". The Jewish leaders announced their intention of sending a letter of protest to Tiberius himself, and there the matter rests.

<u>The Beheading of John</u>

The Rome-bound ship <u>Sagittarius</u> (240 tonnes) is at
present loading cargo at Caesarea before setting out for
Alexandria. A small number of berths are available and
early application should be made direct to the captain.
The sailing date is as yet uncertain and depends on the
weather, but it is expected to be within the week.
Passengers for Alexandria should expect a journey of
about three weeks, while those for Rome will probably
arrive in four months.

Stay tuned to your local radio for evening music. The
late news will be at 11 o'clock.
Good evening!

(Station music
and fade out)

A rocky path leading to the Mount of Olives

Evening News Bulletin III

PALM SUNDAY

Newscaster

Reporter, Jonathan ben Etchel

Roman Officer, Legate Lucius Vitellius

Galilean Jew, Barsabus Justus

Greek Merchant, Popygos

Voice in Crowd

Crowd

(Fade in station music ....)

NEWSCASTER This is Radio Jerusalem. And once again we have unmistakable evidence of the makings of another hectic Passover Week in and around our city. As always, today has been marked by noisy preparations on every hand. At the small arena south of the city athletes have been warming up for the week's events - footracing, discus, javelin, wrestling - much to the delight of the usual crowds of admiring youngsters.
Oh! And despite recent speculation on the subject, there will be no gladiatorial bouts, or even exhibitions. Bloodshed is still strictly forbidden.
As the day has gone on the arena itself has become progressively the centre of almost another city - a city of booths and tents, which are in their great variety the property of travelling entertainers, many of them from far places. They include magicians, we found, from India, pygmies from Africa and Syrian fortune-tellers. Of course there are the inevitable gambling wheels and other games of chance being set up. There are innumerable booths dispensing sweet beverages, decorated figs and exotic confections - just now, a source of wonder and excitement

mainly for the children, but from tomorrow onwards, a
spectacle and a spending spree for their elders.
Their elders today are already immersed in the sale
of pottery, rugs, shawls, assorted homespun, sandals,
saddles, all sorts of ornaments in leather, wood and
silver. Such serious trade soon gets under way, and
mostly downtown.
The usual detachments of Roman soldiery from the forts
at Capernaum, Caesarea, Joppa and Minoa are due in the
city before tomorrow's dawn. No doubt we can look forward to a week of colourful uniformed displays, as
worthy as ever of the Procurator's authority, with special
drill routines in the vicinity of the Temple! The first of
these visiting detachments completed their three-day
journey from Minoa this morning. Some one hundred men
under their new Commander-in-Chief, Legate Lucius
Vitellius, entered the city early today along with some of
the thousands of pilgrims. Jonathan ben Etchel, now
with me in the studio, was out and about early to meet
them. Jonathan?

REPORTER   Yes, as they broke night camp on the approach road, I
                asked the Commander if this was his first visit to
                Jerusalem:

                (Fade in caravan noises - tramping, carts,
                soldiers' accoutrements, horses)

COMMANDER   It is. I arrived in your country only ten days ago. I'm
                looking forward to observing this week's festival.

REPORTER   May I ask about your first impressions on sighting our
                city?

COMMANDER   Since dawn this morning I have been amazed at the tide
                of traffic on the highway - such processions of heavily
                laden camels, long trains of pack-asses with their
                clumsy burdens, and all those men, women, children,
                and slaves, all carrying bundles, baskets, boxes of
                every conceivable shape and size. No wonder this
                pestilential dust rolls so high!

<u>Palm Sunday</u>

REPORTER   Is all this so strange, sir? What about the even greater crowds at your Roman festivals?

COMMANDER   Ah! Truly, in Rome, on a feast-day there's plenty of rough jostling and all manner of rudeness in the great crowds. Arrogant charioteers think nothing of driving their broad iron wheels over the bare feet of children. People on foot treat one another with almost incredible discourtesy. Why, for some fellows a favourite method of making way through a crowd is to dive in with both hands full of mud and filth scooped up from the street. Huh! few care to debate the right of way with these ruffians. No, Rome never won any prizes for the politeness of her gala-day multitudes!

REPORTER   I see. It's the sober behaviour of the Jerusalem pilgrims that amazes you, sir?

COMMANDER   Yes .... and no! You use "sober" as if it's a virtue! To me it seems unhealthy - unnatural! I mean, in spite of her forthright brutality, Rome - on such occasions - is hilarious! Her crowds sing, they cheer, they laugh. I grant you they're mischievous and vulgar, but they're merry! Now this pilgrim throng today? No laughter there! Such a tense, impassioned multitude. That voice - a guttural murmur as if each man is bewailing his own distresses, and all are indifferent to the mumbled yearnings of their neighbours.
Oh! No! There's something almost terrifying about all that obvious earnestness! Let me tell you, not for all the wealth in the world would a Roman make such public display of <u>his</u> private griefs and longings - never!

(Fade out caravan noises)

NEWSCASTER   Well, it's always interesting to hear a stranger's first impressions of our city. I wonder what Legate Vitellius would have made of the demonstration - or whatever it was - on that same road a little later. Jonathan?

REPORTER   I'd no sooner entered the city with the Minoa detachment - quite uneventfully, I may add - when the buzz began

33

about some excitement back on the road. I hurried back and soon encountered some irate residents taking a very poor view of having had all the palms uprooted from their borders and strewn over the road. What a mess! Apparently the incident had started with some sort of procession on the fork road down from Bethany. According to one fellow, "It was like a sharp breeze sweeping through the sluggish swollen stream of pilgrims." Suddenly, he said, men were tossing their packs into the arms of their already overburdened children, breaking loose from their families, and racing across to the Bethany road. Apparently there was shouting and cheering, growing quickly into a concerted reiterated cry. Another onlooker insisted the multitude was in a frenzy as it screamed. Certainly all the evidence points to a pretty hectic situation while it lasted – must have been a bit rough at times. I managed to make some sense of it when I found one very interested spectator who'd viewed it from a good vantage point – up a roadside tree! Barsabas Justus was his name, a robust fellow from the country (Sepphora I think he said). He struck me as being nobody's fool. I asked him how it started:

(Fade in street noises, with bleating sheep)

JUSTUS   It was the yelling that first struck me. Sounded like some boisterous party. But it spread down the line, shouting about a "king". Didn't make sense really!

REPORTER   You reckoned there was someone with them who wanted to be a king – was that it?

JUSTUS   Looked like it. However, as they came nearer there were unmistakable cries of, "Messiah!"

REPORTER   Ah – quite – well we expect that sort of thing on these occasions, don't we?

JUSTUS   Then I caught sight of him ...

REPORTER   The fellow they were shouting about? Could you describe him for us?

<u>Palm Sunday</u>

JUSTUS   Well, it's not easy. There was a tight little circle left
               open in the sort of procession, and on a shaggy white
               donkey sat a brown-haired, bare-headed, well-favoured
               Jew.

REPORTER   Dressed up, was he?

JUSTUS   No. In fact, it looked more like an impromptu "do" to
               me. He had on a simple brown mantle, no decorations.

REPORTER   What about his companions?

JUSTUS   Only a handful that I could see, ordinary enough country
               fellows by the look of them, and not too happy about the
               way their honoured friend was measuring up to the
               occasion, I'd say.

REPORTER   How do you mean?

JUSTUS   Well, instead of receiving the applause with an air of
               triumph – or even of satisfaction – the man on the
               donkey seemed sad about the whole affair. Looked as if
               he'd gladly have none of it!

REPORTER   Was he an old man?

JUSTUS   (rather remote)   No. Not very ....

REPORTER   What did he really look like?

JUSTUS   (vaguely)   I don't know ....

REPORTER   Was he anything like a king?

JUSTUS   (ignoring last question: sort-of-soliloquy)   Strange!
               There was a moment when suddenly my heart was
               pounding – my mouth was probably open too. They'd
               stopped below me. He straightened up on his donkey.
               Those eyes! – full of a sort of wistful compassion, for
               everyone. Yet, everyone was shouting – SHOUTING! It
               wasn't the time or place for shouting! This wasn't the
               sort of man you shouted at, or shouted for! Do you
               understand me? Quiet, that's what the moment demanded,
               quiet! Quiet!!
               (thoughtful pause)   Those eyes!

35

<u>Palm Sunday</u>

REPORTER   (after respectful pause)   Did you see him close up?

JUSTUS   (vaguely)   Y-e-s ....

REPORTER   Would you say he was crazy?

JUSTUS   (not so vague)   N-o ....

REPORTER   A king then?

JUSTUS   No.   (definitely)   Not a king!

REPORTER   Then how <u>would</u> <u>you</u> describe him?

JUSTUS   I don't know - but -   (positively)   he struck me as something more important than a king!

(Fade out street noises)

REPORTER   Subsequent enquiries revealed that the man on the white donkey was Jesus of Nazareth, about whom there has been so much talk, so many rumours these past two years. And it must be admitted that this morning's demonstration hasn't helped to clarify what he's up to. One minute there's this royal procession, the next, the whole thing's fizzled out! Is the man a complete fool, or is he superlatively courageous? For the white donkey entry <u>was</u> an act of glorious defiance.
When you consider the price already on this Jesus' head, if he had to come into Jerusalem, what would have been more natural than to slip in unseen to some pre-arranged hideout? Instead, he appears to have gone out of his way to focus massive attention upon himself. The sheer courage of it only adds to the mystery of who this Jesus thinks he is, and what he's doing!
The next report we received of him was a rumpus mid-afternoon - sheer defiance again - in the Temple itself!
Outside the Temple I found a Greek Merchant, Popygos, revelling in his version of the incident:

(Fade in background market sounds)

POPYGOS   What happened? Plenty! You see, the Temple is where the people make sacrifices - buy animals and burn them.

36

Nasty mess, bad smell, but their god seems to like it.
So, the loggia - or whatever they call it - is crowded full
of animals for sale. The people bring their money and
the money-changers, just inside the door, convert it into
Temple money. "Convert".   (laughing)   They say
these bankers make a bomb.

CROWD

Get on with it.
Stop mucking about.
Tell us what happened.

POPYGOS

All right, all right. There's this great arcaded court, all
marble - magnificent - and it's full of calves and sheep
and pigeons. Just imagine the scene. Oh. But, you
can't imagine the smell - phew. Stinks to high heaven.
Well, this Jesus came in and took one look. Didn't like
what he saw - not one little bit he didn't, so, <u>did he</u>
<u>sort it out</u>?

(He laughs long and loud)

CROWD

Never, not him.
How could he?
What are you saying?
You've got the wrong bloke.
Jesus is not that sort of fellow.

POPYGOS

Oh, yes, he did. Maybe he <u>doesn't</u> look the type, but
I'm telling you. That Jesus took a whip, and with a
Crash. a Lash. a Zip. and a Slash. he really laid
about him, at the same time flaying them with his tongue.
"God's Temple should be a house of prayer for all nations,
but <u>you</u>," he said, "YOU have turned it into a thieves'
kitchen."
Oh.   (laughing)   I liked that - "a thieves' kitchen." -
and out they tumbled - marvellous. - <u>calves</u> and <u>priests</u>
and <u>sheep</u> and <u>bankers</u>, and the air full of pigeons and
flying feathers.   (rocking with laughter)   And as if
that wasn't enough, over went the money tables - Jesus
again - money all over the floor, shekels, drachma,
denarii, big money, little money, good money, bad

money, and some of the stall-holders down on their hands and knees scrabbling after it!
What a sight! I wouldn't have missed it for anything!

VOICE   (ringing out)   You can laugh, but there's talk already of charging this same Jesus with "defiling the Temple", and <u>that</u> could be serious!

POPYGOS   You must be joking, friend. How can anyone defile a Temple that's already been turned into a stable?

(General laughter, and fade out)

REPORTER   As our regular listeners will know we are <u>still</u> not allowed to <u>record</u> in the Temple. But I went on in, and there was Jesus bar Joseph. Such nerve you've got to admire! He was preaching. I'm no authority in this field, but I can tell you the people hung upon his every word. He asked them if they <u>really</u> knew where they were?

"Doesn't your inside leap, with feeling near to God, in <u>his</u> dwelling? Feel it," he said, "f-e-e-l the awe with which our forefathers built this great Temple in praise of Almighty God. Each pillar is a prayer. The floor beneath your feet is a work of devotion! But this generation SPITS upon it! And OUR faith? It droops, it cowers pitifully."
I'm afraid I do the man little justice in trying to report something of his message. It is not possible to imitate the power with which he invests his words, <u>especially</u> when he's replying to hecklers and questions meant to entrap him!
"Give us a sign!" one heckler cried, others took it up, and a Temple official challenged, "Yes, give us a sign if you are from God, I said, <u>if</u>!"
"Come here." Jesus beckoned him over. Out he came. "A bit closer. Now, <u>you</u> <u>want</u> <u>a</u> <u>sign</u>?" said Jesus. (crescendo) "How about a THUNDERBOLT (bitingly). Let me crackle some flames through your limbs, Temple official, eh?" The crowd simply rocked with laughter to see that smart alec official scuttle away. And Jesus

wrapped that one up with: "Only a godless generation asks for a sign."
But straightway somebody else called out: "Master, should we pay taxes to the Romans? <u>You</u> tell us what to do, Master."
Jesus seemed amused with this one. "All right," he said, "have you got a coin? Come on, come on, a coin. Thanks. Now, who's head is this on the coin?"
"Caesar's!" came the answer all round.
"Well," said Jesus, "you give to Caesar what belongs to Caesar, and you give to God what belongs to God. And be done with your stupid questions!" How the priests squirmed, the Temple hecklers cringed, and the people loved every minute of it. Yet all this was as nothing compared with the scenes when the blind and the sick and the lame pressed upon this same Jesus to be healed. <u>And</u> <u>they</u> <u>were</u>!
I doubt whether the Temple has ever before echoed such wild mouthings and clamour, and through it all a sort of haunting chant, "God save the Son of David! God save the Son of David!" No wonder highly indignant priests confronted Jesus with, "Just listen to what these children are saying." And his parting shot was, "Haven't you ever read the words, 'Out of the mouths of babes and sucklings'?"

NEWSCASTER Thank you, Jonathan ben Etchel. Altogether it looks like being as lively a Passover Week as the city has ever seen – a week when, even more than usual, Radio Jerusalem will be out and about covering the sports, entertainments, ceremonies, parades, in fact, all events of interest and excitement. So stay tuned to your very own radio station on 94.6 metres.
Until our late news at 11 o'clock,
            good evening!

            (Station music
            and fade out)

Recently excavated in Caesarea, a marble tablet with the name of
Pontius Pilate, Roman Governor of Judaea in Jesus' time

Evening News Bulletin IV

<u>GOOD FRIDAY</u>

Newscaster

Reporter, Jonathan ben Etchel

1st Reveller

2nd Reveller

3rd Reveller

Caiaphas, High Priest

Herod's Chamberlain

Pontius Pilate

Merchant, elderly Athenian

1st Man

2nd Man, Simon Cyrene

1st Woman

2nd Woman

1st Soldier   )
2nd Soldier   )   Roman
3rd Soldier   )   Crucifixion
Officer   )   Squad

(Fade in station music ....)

NEWSCASTER   This is Radio Jerusalem.
Our main news this evening is right here in Jerusalem.
The political unrest that has bedevilled the city this
Passover Week came to a head today with the crucifixion
of Jesus bar Joseph, a religious leader. He was arrested
late last night and immediately brought to trial before the

<u>Good Friday</u>

Jewish priests.   Later, before Pontius Pilate, the Roman Governor, he was condemned to death. Radio Jerusalem reporter, Jonathan ben Etchel, has been out and about in the city all day, and we go over to him now for more details of the day's happenings.

(Fade in background noise of sinister wind)

REPORTER   And what a day! At this moment I am standing at the foot of the Hill of Golgotha. The crowds have gone, and as the shadows lengthened in the setting sun a while ago, three crosses stood out starkly on the hill-top. Now they make an eerie picture against the evening sky. But let's go back to the beginning of an unforgettable twenty-four hours, with its storm and earthquake, the arrest of the revolutionary, Jesus, and his crucifixion. Out on the streets early this morning I encountered lots of excited folk, some of them, I suspect, all-night revellers. I questioned one such group:

(Change sound effects to street noises – people walking about)

Gentlemen, may I ask you if you have seen anything of this man Jesus who was arrested last night?

1st REVELLER   You mean that crazy carpenter from somewhere in Galilee?

2nd REVELLER   I'll say he's crazy. Been tried for disturbing the peace and exciting the people to revolt.

1st REVELLER   They say he was violent in the Temple a few days ago. Chased the sacrificial animals out into the street, upset the money-tills, and fairly shouted down the holy place as a den of robbers.

2nd REVELLER   (laughingly)   What a sight! Wish we'd been in time for <u>that</u> performance.

3rd REVELLER   Fancy telling them to their face they're a lot of thieves! And he's right, oh, yes!

1st REVELLER   Maybe, but it's asking for trouble to say so straight out in public – crazy – and yet ....   (continues more

thoughtfully)   something peculiar about him. I mean,
look what they did – arrested him last night. Straight up
before old Annas, who used to be High Priest. Then
Caiaphas, the present High Priest. And Pilate, then
Herod, and ...

REPORTER   You seem to know a lot about it!

2nd REVELLER   Ah well, you see, sir, a few of us were – er – doing the
holy city by moonlight, if you know what I mean.

3rd REVELLER   Fact is, we ran into this mob shortly after midnight, and
tagged along. Seemed to be the only entertainment
going. We'd tried everything else, and – well – we
were a bit merry, like!

REPORTER   Er – quite – but please go on with what you can remember.

1st REVELLER   Well, we went to the trials, one after the other. Couldn't
understand much of what was said – so much shrieking
in Aramaic – not in the mood anyway. But I can tell you
this, that Temple mob was set on having the fellow put
to death.

REPORTER   For what happened at the Temple?

1st REVELLER   I suppose so.

3rd REVELLER   There's more to it than that, though!

REPORTER   In what way?

3rd REVELLER   Something, well, odd about the man himself. Witnesses
said that in the Temple he acted as if he owned the place.
At old man Annas' house last night I'm blowed if he didn't
go on as if it was <u>his</u> house. At Caiaphas' palace, everybody seemed to be on trial, except this Jesus.

2nd REVELLER   Come off it! You don't know what you are saying.

3rd REVELLER   NO? Just you think back to Pilate's courtyard. Who was
the only cool one in that mob? Go on, admit it, the
fellow Jesus. Why, anyone might have thought <u>he</u> was in
<u>command</u>, instead of being the prisoner. And I'll tell
you something else, I reckon Pilate felt it too.

1st and 2nd) REVELLERS) together)	Rubbish! Nonsense! Get lost! (etc.) Come away with you, that's the wine talking.

(Change sound effects, and fade in
wind noises)

REPORTER   It would appear that this Jesus was arrested in the garden of Gethsemane about 11 o'clock last night on the orders of Caiaphas, the High Priest. After some sort of preliminary examination by Annas, he was taken to Caiaphas and an informal sitting of the Sanhedrin soon after midnight. Incidentally, there are those who say that such meetings during the night are illegal! Just what happened there is not very clear – a profusion of witnesses seems to have led to such confusion of testimonies that the exact nature of the offences with which Jesus was charged remains disturbingly vague.
Some hours elapsed before Caiaphas agreed to be interviewed at his palace:

(Fade out wind, fade in large room effect)

CAIAPHAS   I speak for the Sanhedrin as well as myself when I say that we wish it to be clearly understood that no one regretted the necessity for the death penalty more than we did. And straightaway, I should like to take this opportunity to express our most sincere sympathy with the relatives of the crucified man.
In principle we are all of us opposed to the death penalty. It is unlawful for us to shed blood. Even so we do have the Law for the protection of the general good, and it must be administered, however painful the duty for those of us responsible for its execution. Society must be protected.

REPORTER   My Lord Caiaphas, are you saying that this man was a danger to the nation?

CAIAPHAS   No doubt about it. For years this fellow has flaunted our authority. This week his behaviour has been disgraceful, and under cross-examination he not only spoke frantically about destroying the Temple and re-building it, but made the utterly blasphemous claim to be the Son of God. Of course, all good Jews await the coming of the <u>true</u> Messiah. Meanwhile, we who are called to be responsible for the spiritual well-being of our people have no more important task than that of protecting their minds from perversion, especially perversion by false messiahs.

REPORTER   And you were <u>quite</u> <u>certain</u> that Jesus was not the true Messiah?

CAIAPHAS   Quite certain. Why, the man's a Galilean!

REPORTER   Was the Sanhedrin's verdict unanimous, my Lord?

CAIAPHAS   (peevishly)   Of course!

REPORTER   Isn't it true, your Grace, that the Sanhedrin was not fully representative, and that Nicodemus voted against the majority?

CAIAPHAS   (somewhat cagily)   Ah well - er - this <u>was</u> an emergency session. And Nicodemus! You know how it is, there's always the odd one who hasn't the courage to face up to an issue when a decision is vital.   (more confidently) This I <u>can</u> say. I have the warmest support of all the <u>responsible</u> members in the very firm line I felt it necessary to take.

(Fade out large room effect, fade in wind)

REPORTER   In accordance with Roman Law, the High Priest next sent Jesus to the Roman Governor for official ratification of the sentence. Apparently this did not go strictly according to plan. Perhaps Governor Pilate's natural irritation at the earliness of the hour was a factor. And we understand his wife, Lady Claudia, had some strong views on the subject. Be that as it may, the case was referred to King Herod, the Tetrarch of Galilee. At the palace His Majesty's Court Chamberlain was gracious enough to answer a few questions.

(Fade out wind, fade in music in background)

Lord Chamberlain, you were present at the interrogation of Jesus bar Joseph?

CHAMBERLAIN Yes, of course, and I must say, it was a very disappointing affair!

REPORTER How? Disappointing?

CHAMBERLAIN As messiahs go this fellow was decidedly below par. After all the sensational reports about the fellow, King Herod - and I may say the rest of us too - had high hopes that this Jesus would work a few miracles. You know, heal a cripple or two, perhaps even raise somebody from the dead. We all expected something of the sort, but the fellow simply wouldn't play. Couldn't even get a word out of him.

REPORTER You mean he didn't even speak up in his own defence?

CHAMBERLAIN Not a single word. Just stood there and stared us all straight back in the eye. A bit off-putting it was!

REPORTER Then what?

CHAMBERLAIN Ah, well, the whole thing was threatening to become a little embarrassing. But King Herod has a way with him - dressed this Jesus up as a mock-king, with some frightfully amusing trimmings, like the crown made up of thorns. So whimsical! Then the King sent him back to Pilate.

REPORTER What, all the way back through the streets dressed like a comic king?

CHAMBERLAIN Of course, all part of King Herod's cleverness. The Tetrarch reckons that the best way to control excitable people like the Jews, especially at festival times, when these messiahs are doing their stuff, is to provide some comic relief - nothing like a good laugh to restore a sense of proportion. Keeps the people out of mischief. Believe me, this was as funny a thing as King Herod's ever done.

(Fade out music, fade in wind again)

REPORTER	The joke, if there was one in this situation, seems to have misfired. Back before Pilate again, Jesus stood his final trial. It was some hours later before I was able to ask the Governor for his account of the proceedings:

(Fade out wind, fade in marching soldier noises off, or hollow "museum" effect)

PILATE	The man was a fanatic, wasn't he? Must have been. He claimed, in some sense or another, to be the King of the Jews. Do you know that it was this which forced High Priest Caiaphas to acknowledge in public that he and his like have no king but Caesar? I thought he would choke on the words. Ironic isn't it?

REPORTER	Your excellency, can you be more precise about this man's claim to be a king? What _is_ the truth about him?

PILATE	Truth? You may well ask. Who knows? I must admit he didn't measure up to the usual picture of a political revolutionary. All the same he impressed me, simply as a _man_.

REPORTER	What was the significance of washing your hands in the sight of the crowd as you pronounced the death sentence?

PILATE	A less drastic punishment would have been more to my taste so I made it clear that I accepted no responsibility for what was to be done. In effect this was not really a Roman affair, and in such cases it is policy to let the will of the people prevail.

REPORTER	And your sentence was in line with public opinion?

PILATE	There was no doubt about that! It was so obvious as to be frightening. The crowd in the court was so extraordinarily excited - shouting, screaming, baying like animals for this man's blood. I wouldn't want to see or hear such a crowd ever again.

REPORTER	Would I be right, your excellency, in describing this as an _unusual_ case?

PILATE	(reflectively)	Yes, it certainly was - unusual trial, unusual decision, unusual punishment. That fellow was such an unusual man!

REPORTER   Is that why you had written over his cross,
"Jesus of Nazareth, King of the Jews"?
For wasn't that the very claim for which he was executed?

PILATE   (more himself)   Ah! The Jews didn't like that, didn't like it at all. Wanted me to remove it. I refused.

REPORTER   Why?

PILATE   (strongly)   It's high time they learned that a Roman Governor is not a person to be dictated to!

   (Fade out soldier noises, fade in sinister
   wind again)

REPORTER   If the trials and torturings of Jesus were pushed through during the night in the hope of avoiding publicity, the plan miscarried markedly. This has been the one topic of excitement in every part of the city today. I asked an old Athenian spice merchant, a regular visitor to Jerusalem, for his impressions of the day.

   (Fade out wind, fade in loud market and
   animal effects)

MERCHANT   I have been making this trip for three and twenty years. It gets worse every time, less and less trade, always some big squabble in this Passover Week to keep my best customers from coming for their cloves and cinnamon.

REPORTER   Has it always been like this?

MERCHANT   I can remember a time when there weren't so many rackets. Look at this business in the Temple the other day. Time was when country folk came in for the Passover bringing a dove in a cage if they were poor, or a lamb or calf if they could afford it. That was for the Temple, burnt offerings, they say. Seems the Temple officials got smart, discovered small blemishes or warts on the lamb offered - not good enough - but they could take the damaged lamb in return for a good one, <u>plus</u> a cash payment for the difference. Then the so-called blemished lamb was all ready to sell as perfect to the next customer!

REPORTER   No wonder somebody has at last objected to such dirty trading.

MERCHANT   Quite - but it won't do any good in the long run. Hasn't done <u>him</u> any good, has it? And it's all so bad for business.

             (Interruption by a "man in the street")

1st MAN   Business? Who cares about business? This is a festival, anything that's exciting is welcome.

REPORTER   Ah! <u>You've</u> seen something of this Jesus?

1st MAN   Plenty. Been like a circus. 'Course it all started last Sunday when this Nazarene came in on a shaggy white donkey. Me and the wife got caught up in the crowd, tearing off branches of palm and throwing them in front of him. We all shouted "Hosannah". What a start to the week - great fun! That was last Sunday. Different today. Same fellow, seems he's been causing the bosses a lot of trouble. Today it wasn't "Hosannah", but "Crucify".

REPORTER   And what did you do about it?

1st MAN   Well, what do you think? Joined in, had a jolly good shout of "Crucify" with the rest of 'em.

REPORTER   Isn't that a terrible thing to be shouting?

1st MAN   They was all doin' it! No sense in being awkward. I mean it's only a bit of fun, everybody havin' a ball shouting their heads off. It's not going to hurt anyone, is it?

REPORTER   But .... Ah, excuse me!   (shouting)   Sir, you sir! Am I right in thinking that you carried the cross for the man Jesus?

2nd MAN   Yes, that's right.

<u>Good Friday</u>

REPORTER   You are one of his followers?

2nd MAN   Oh no! Never saw him before today. I'm just visiting
               Jerusalem. I'm a Greek from Cyrene.

REPORTER   Then how did you come to carry his cross?

2nd MAN   I understand it is normal practice for these criminals to
               carry their own crosses, but this man was in poor shape
               physically, beaten up something cruel, I'd say. The
               cross was more than he could manage, though I must say
               he didn't seem willing to give up. Anyhow, they picked
               on a big chap - who happened to be me - and made me
               carry it.

REPORTER   Didn't you object to this?

2nd MAN   As a matter of fact I'd already told the soldiers what I
               thought of their behaviour.   (pause)   No! I didn't
               object then.

REPORTER   Are you saying you were pleased to have helped this
               Jesus?

2nd MAN   Well, y-e-s .... yes, I was.

               (Vehement interruption by woman)

1st WOMAN   Serves you right if you'd been strung up with him!

REPORTER   I take it you had no sympathy for Jesus, Ma'am?

2nd WOMAN   Sympathy! For a nobody who's always causing trouble,
               then comes here and calls himself the Messiah? You
               must be joking!

REPORTER   He's not the first to call himself Messiah. Surely
               crucifying him for it is a bit drastic.

1st WOMAN   No, he was dangerous. Should have been stopped long
               ago. I've no patience with blasphemy. He asked for it,
               he got it, so there!

REPORTER   They say he did a lot of good, healings and so on?

2nd WOMAN   They <u>say</u>! Huh, yes, they <u>say</u> he worked miracles, but

I never saw him do anything but talk. Talk! Anybody
can talk!

1st WOMAN   Anyhow, we're bound to know the real Messiah when he
comes. Stands to reason, don't it?

(Fade out market noises, fade in sinister
wind again)

REPORTER   The complete darkness at 3 o'clock this afternoon, some
say at the very moment Jesus died, was not a subject
anyone cared to discuss. But soon afterwards I talked
with the soldiers of the crucifixion party and asked their
impressions of the execution.

(Fade out wind, fade in storm and dice-playing
sound effects)

1st SOLDIER   That middle one of the three went on a bit. Thought he'd
had it more than once, then suddenly he was crying out
again.   (Dice thrown)

2nd SOLDIER   3 and 4 - 7!   (soldiers react)

REPORTER   What did he say?

3rd SOLDIER   Heaven knows - we don't know the lingo. Once somebody said he called out he was thirsty. I filled a sponge
with the usual vinegar - it has some sort of drug in it -
and put it up to his mouth. But he wouldn't touch it, as
thirsty as he was. I don't rightly understand what he's
up there for, but he was no coward.

REPORTER   And what was <u>your</u> impression of this Jesus, Sir?

OFFICER   Strange, very strange! Not much to say for himself, but
a fighter, he might have been a Roman. He was fighting
to the end, I'm sure of that. Raised his head and called
out powerfully.

REPORTER   Saying what?

OFFICER   Haven't a clue.   (Dice thrown again)   But it was the
way he said it. They told me that once he called on his
god to forgive us, and he looked straight at me as he

said it. I'm afraid I'm not likely to forget that look in a hurry.   (Dice thrown)

2nd SOLDIER   Huh - double one!

(Soldiers laugh - fade from laughter to wind effect only)

REPORTER   Now, as I speak to you, the Hill of Golgotha is deserted. The body of Jesus has been taken down from the cross, presumably by some of his followers, and in that connection I have to admit that I haven't been able to find a single follower of Jesus anywhere today. They seem to have disappeared completely from the moment of his arrest last night. Strange!
I understand that the body is to be buried in the tomb of a wealthy Pharisee, Joseph of Arimathea.
So another lonely man has thrown away his life and there is nothing but a bloodstained cross to show for his audacious courage.
And as I hand you back to the studio, all I can say is - what a price to pay for a brief and fruitless attack on wickedness.

(Fade out wind effect)

NEWSCASTER   Thank you, Jonathan ben Etchel.
The rest of the news.
The Emperor Tiberius is leaving Rome for the island of Capri, in the Bay of Naples. According to our Rome correspondent Emperor Tiberius may have presided over his last Imperial Cabinet in Rome itself. The Emperor says he is tired of having to rule, and at the age of 67 proposes to find some peace and solitude on Capri.
Unconfirmed reports suggest that fear of assassination is a further reason for the Emperor's decision.
The amphitheatre in Fidenae is reported to have collapsed and many thousands are feared buried in the ruins. We expect to have more details of this disaster in the late news.
Apicius, most famous of Rome's cooks and compiler of a

recent luxury cookery book, has invented a new recipe
for an egg dish which he calls an "omelette". Already
renowned for his cooking of pigs' livers and flamingo
tongues, Apicius now offers a very simple dish in which
eggs are beaten and mixed with water, herbs, and spices
before being fried in a flat pan. To this mixture Apicius
adds chopped meats and vegetables, and in this way he
combines both the flavours to produce a quick and
appetising savoury.
And on that spicy note, until the late news at 11 o'clock,
good evening!

(Station music
and fade out)

Evening News Bulletin V

<u>EASTER DAY</u>

Newscaster

Reporter, Jonathan ben Etchel

Mary Magdala

Caiaphas, High Priest

Disciple, Thomas

Cleopas, another Disciple

Crowd

(Fade in station music ....)

NEWSCASTER   This is Radio Jerusalem, on a day when <u>all</u> else has
given way to the greatest sensation ever! For right here
in Jerusalem a man, after death and burial, is reported
ALIVE!
It sound unbelievable, impossible. Not surprisingly,
then, news agencies and radio lines everywhere are
taking their headlines from <u>us</u> today.
So before I hand you over to Jonathan ben Etchel for on-
the-spot reports, here's a recap of earlier bulletins today
with the facts as they have come into us from responsible
eye-witnesses. First, the man Jesus bar Joseph did <u>not</u>
die from natural causes, he was executed.
Soldiers of the execution party report the job was done
efficiently, and a spear through the heart finished him
off. The victim was buried in a hewn rock grave in a
public place.
A guard was set over the grave because of rumours of
some plot to abduct the body.
Then, thirty-six hours after the sealing of the grave
entrance - that is, at dawn today - the grave was discovered empty. The door had been removed. This

afternoon, some of the deceased's - well, er - some of
this man's friends have sworn that he appeared to them
and talked with them freely. In fairness to them perhaps
we ought to add that they did seem scared stiff over the
whole business! Jonathan?

REPORTER   By all ordinary standards of human reasoning any mystery
attaching to the person of Jesus of Nazareth ought to
have ended with his death and burial on Friday. And
nothing could be more certain than that he <u>did</u> die, and
he <u>was</u> given a respectful burial.
Today however, an utterly unbelievable situation builds
up. Yes, with every new report, with each fresh angle,
it builds up to something that would be dismissed as
quite incredible, but for one thing - the obvious sincerity,
the consistency, and the genuine surprise of the men and
women involved. And <u>there</u> is a striking feature of this
whole affair. As I reported on Friday evening, I hadn't
been able to locate a single supporter of Jesus, but I
failed to take into account the womenfolk! For, believe
it or not, the active and mobile section of Jesus'
followers within Jerusalem since his arrest Thursday
evening has been limited to a few women. Indeed, it is
no exaggeration to say that the whole brunt of the crisis
which descended so suddenly on the Jesus' party was
borne by three or four women!
Cut off from effective communication with their friends,
these women sustained the full impact of the catastrophe,
alone. And the prime mover in this group seems to have
been Mary Magdala. Certainly she was the first to raise
the cry of - er - resurrection this morning. At mid-
morning she was kind enough to comment for us.

(Fade in house sounds - shuffling, crockery,
hushed voices, perhaps weeping)

MARY   .... the shock, heart-breaking. We still had - the last
rites - anointing, you know. And yesterday was the
Sabbath ....   (brighter) This morning there were
birds, birds singing!

<u>Easter Day</u>

REPORTER   So it was hardly light, Mary, when you ventured on to
the streets this morning?

MARY   Yes. We didn't want to be seen, we were still frightened.
Mary, the mother of James, and Salome were marvellous
really. Even managed a joke about how we were going to
move that hefty stone from the tomb entrance. Seemed
silly going at all, just three women, with that great
thing in the way.   (feelingly)   But we had to!

     (Pause)

REPORTER   And when you reached the tomb, it was light?

MARY   Yes, almost ...   (anguished)   the clay seals were
broken, the stone was rolled away. How? We, I, I
don't know how long we stood - huddled together, staring.
We did go in. He, he wasn't there! Our Lord wasn't
there!
Then suddenly this young man, standing, all in white.
Odd? He spoke: "You're looking for Jesus," he said.
"He's risen, he's not here. "   (weeping)

REPORTER   (softly)   Mary, can you recall? Did this - er - person,
say anything more?

MARY   I - we - we were too terrified to move. Something? Yes,
"Go and tell the disciples," Oh! "And Peter." Somehow,
we were outside again, stumbling away. Mary and
Salome, they're older, you know. They pushed me on. I
don't remember anything else until I burst in here,
gasping out my news.

REPORTER   Some of the disciples were here then?

MARY   Oh, yes, Peter and John! They were furious, rushed off
madly. I don't know why, but I went after them. They
saw the empty tomb, dashed off somewhere else. Left
me in the garden, and .... and ....   (long pause)

REPORTER   (softly)   What was it, Mary?

MARY   (bursts out with)   It's no good, I can't describe it, I
can't explain it! But he came to me. Jesus <u>was</u> there!

A garden tomb

<u>Easter Day</u>

He was standing looking at me. He called me - it was
<u>his</u> voice, I am certain.
"Mary," he said, "Mary."

(Fade out house sounds)

REPORTER   By noon this story was public property. On the streets
explanation was being met with counter-explanation,
charge met by counter-charge. Vulgar wranglings and
sinister suggestion were bandied around freely.
Then it was announced that there was to be a special
council of the Sanhedrin. This encouraged some to
expect an explanation, perhaps a conclusive explanation.
Obviously the emergency meeting was concerned with
this renewal of public interest in Jesus of Nazareth.
However, it proved to be a longer session than we
reporters anticipated. We'd stood around most of the
afternoon before the heavily guarded doors were eventually thrown open and the High Priest came out onto the
steps to read a prepared statement:

(Fade in sounds of a crowd cheering and
booing, which eventually give way to a hush
as Caiaphas speaks)

CAIAPHAS   The Elders of the Sanhedrin have heard the report of the
Captain and the three temple policemen who were on duty
last night at the tomb of the Nazarene. Due note has
been taken of the fact that these men were detached at
short notice from the Temple Guard who had been on prac-
tically continuous duty since the important arrest on
Thursday night. We have given serious consideration -
very serious consideration - to this detailed report.
Whilst it is not our wish to cast any doubts upon the
loyalty and integrity of any part of our Temple Guard, it
would appear that in the extremities of this additional
onerous task, sheer exhaustion must have overtaken this
otherwise trustworthy guard.   (much more confidently)
Accordingly, I am in <u>no doubt</u> that the simple truth of
this matter of the broken tomb is that at some point
during the night the body was stolen.

<u>Easter Day</u>

<blockquote>(Fade in renewal of sound of crowd shouting
with distinguishable cries of "never", "Lord
Caiaphas", etc.)</blockquote>

REPORTER   (cutting through general outcry with:)   My Lord Caiaphas,
you were gracious enough to comment on Friday's hap-
penings for Radio Jerusalem ....

CAIAPHAS   (interrupting)   You have recorded my statement?

REPORTER   Certainly, Your Grace. But what do you say to this evidence that Jesus of Nazareth has been seen alive today?
And that he spoke to someone?

CAIAPHAS   (contemptuously)   Ridiculous! Vicious and irrespons-
ible nonsense!

REPORTER   That's not how it seemed to me, sir.

CAIAPHAS   Your informant <u>Mary</u> <u>Magdala</u>, oh, yes! I too am well
informed in these matters. This women is a sensual,
brazen creature of the most unsavoury reputation. Evidence, did you say?

REPORTER   You know this woman personally, My Lord?

CAIAPHAS   Not at all, and I have no wish to do so. The reports I
have on her are more than enough for me.

REPORTER   She held an honourable place among the friends of Jesus,
who knew her well.

CAIAPHAS   (sarcastically)   Honourable? Do you know what you
are saying? A notoriously immoral ex-belly-dancer
joins twelve men - and some of them already married -
lives with them on their wanderings in the hill country,
and you talk of honour!

REPORTER   But ....

CAIAPHAS   (cuttingly)   Enough! A man has been executed for blasphemy and treason. He was shabby and poor, a
Nazarene, a drunkard - and you yourself have drawn
attention to the company he kept. He died as he lived,
discredited and without honour.   (With abrupt finality)

<u>Easter Day</u>

(Renewed outcry from crowd – fade out)

REPORTER   Well! Er – nothing more has been seen or heard from the Elders since. Moreover, all efforts to locate the quartet who made up that fateful temple guard have proved fruitless. As one weary reporter said, "Perhaps they're <u>really</u> sleeping it off now!"
On my way back to the studio, among those who asked me for the latest news was a well-favoured Jew – he spoke with a Galilean accent. A matter of minutes later he admitted to having been a follower of Jesus bar Joseph. Preferred not to give his name. That's understandable, I suppose.

(Fade in ordinary street noises)

You've heard what they are saying? Jesus is alive?

DISCIPLE   Yes. Of course, our womenfolk have had a pretty rough time. Can't blame <u>them</u> for such hysterical outbursts. But Peter and John, they're men! I know we've all been through hell this past week, but I didn't expect <u>them</u> to break. I just don't understand them – an empty tomb? Jesus standing there in the room with them, talking like old times? Oh, no!

REPORTER   If I may say so, you seem to be determined <u>not</u> to accept any of this story?

DISCIPLE   N-o-o, I wouldn't say that. But seeing's believing, isn't it? I'm not taking anybody's word on <u>this</u>, not even Peter's or John's. I'd have to see it. I'd have to see <u>him</u> for myself – more than that! Until I've seen those bloodied nail holes in his hands, until I can shove my fingers into that gaping spear-wound in his side, I'll not believe a word of it.

(Fade out street noises)

NEWSCASTER Well, that's the up-to-the-minute news of today's sensation for this news bulletin. Of course, we'll be ....

(Telephone rings)

Excuse me. Yes .... yes .... It's for you, Jonathan, another follower of Jesus. Says it's important and he's calling from Emmaus.

REPORTER   Hello, this is Jonathan ben Etchel.

CLEOPAS   My name is Cleopas. I don't suppose you remember me but we met on one of your "Soundings" programmes, and I thought you should know what happened out here this afternoon.

REPORTER   Cleopas, before you go any further, we _are_ on an open line. This conversation is going out on the air?

CLEOPAS   Oh! I'd like to go on, if I may ....

REPORTER   Certainly, please do.

CLEOPAS   A friend and I walked home from Jerusalem this afternoon. The West road, you know, sun in our eyes all the way, a chance to discuss recent events - dashed hopes, shattered illusions. We hardly noticed that someone joined us, we were so engrossed in our talk, until he asked _what_ we were talking about! I retorted he must be the only man hereabouts completely _unaware_ of what's been going on in Jerusalem. "What things?" he asked. We told him the story of Jesus of Nazareth, his work and his words, his challenge in Jerusalem itself last week, the death sentence, the crucifixion; then today, how some of our women fairly shook us with their story of going to the tomb first thing, not finding the body there and then coming back saying they'd seen a vision of angels who said Jesus was alive, though _we_ hadn't seen him.

REPORTER   And this stranger didn't believe a word of it?

CLEOPAS   On the contrary, beginning with Moses, he worked his way through the prophets interpreting all sorts of texts and quotations connected with the idea of a Messiah.

REPORTER   He was preaching to the converted, wasn't he?

CLEOPAS   As a matter of fact, he accused _us_ of being _dim_ about the whole affair.

<u>Easter Day</u>

REPORTER   He did what?

CLEOPAS   Oh! we didn't mind. We appreciated he was talking
            sense, particularly about the Messiah having to suffer.
            Anyhow we persuaded him to stop off with us for a spot
            of tea.

REPORTER   That's fine, Cleopas, but what was it you rang me about
            especially?

CLEOPAS   This is it. Listen. He picked up a piece of bread, he
            blessed it, he broke it, he handed it around . . . .
            (silence)

REPORTER   Hello? Cleopas, are you still there?

CLEOPAS   (rather uncertainly)   Y-e-s, I'm here . . . .

REPORTER   Go on then, what next?

CLEOPAS   You see, that's it. We-recognised him-as he handed
            us the bread.

REPORTER   You mean . . . . ?

CLEOPAS   That's right, it was Jesus! Then he just went!
            (excitedly - self-critically)   We should have known,
            there he was!

REPORTER   Quite, yes, Cleopas-we understand, and thank you for
            ringing.

            (In background Cleopas continues to say, "We
            should have known", "Didn't our hearts burn
            within us!")
            (Replace telephone)

Make of that what you will. The tables have been turned
today with a vengeance! This Jesus bar Joseph, alive
after death (or whatever) persuades his desolated friends
that his teaching has been the truth. What he said about
a "caring God", a "Father God" takes on new dimensions
in the face of <u>their</u> betrayal and desertion, <u>his</u> dereliction
on the cross, the seeming cold, brutal finality of his
death.

<u>Easter Day</u>

Today, in <u>our</u> city, there <u>is</u> an <u>empty</u> <u>tomb</u>! And whatever tomorrow brings, let alone the future, the seeming
return of this Jesus to continue his mission of love, spot-
lights anew and afresh every single element of the horror
of Friday's Calvary event.

NEWSCASTER   Well, here at Radio Jerusalem we can be relied upon to
follow up this remarkable affair. Why, in the whole
field of news-reporting it must be true to say that this
day's happenings in Jerusalem mark a new era. Never
has there been the like of this before, and if there be
any truth in it, things can never be quite the same again,
can they?
More news at 11 o'clock - until then
                good evening!

        (Station music
        and fade out)

Evening News Bulletin VI

PENTECOST

Newscaster

Reporter, Jonathan ben Etchel

Simon Cyrene

1st Bystander

2nd Bystander

1st Woman

2nd Woman

Pharisee

Saul of Tarsus

Simon Peter

Caiaphas, High Priest

Priests

(Fade in station music ....)

NEWSCASTER This is Radio Jerusalem.
For another year Pentecost has proved itself the gayest
occasion of the Jewish year. Many an oldster tells how
this day used to be a solemn and quiet occasion, but
nowadays Pentecost is the festival of joyous music,
colourful processions and dancing in the streets – a gala
day, a fitting mark to the end of a good barley harvest.
All day – and a beautifully warm summer's day it has
been – Jerusalem's streets have swarmed with crowds in
a state of happy confusion. Very early the city's gates
were adorned with bright bunting and banners, booths
and bazaars decorated with garlands of mid-summer
flowers. Confectioners, busy over their hot braziers,

have filled the air with tantalising aromas of mint and anise. The usual harpists and pipers discordantly competed with begging minstrels for the favours of fun-seeking holiday-makers.

On the other hand, there have been, as usual, the more serious-minded visitors to our city for the celebrated Pentecost camel-auction, conducted by Arabians, breeders of incomparable camels. The day is not least remarkable in that Jews and Arabs manage to put aside their differences for twenty-four hours in such trade.

So another Day of Pentecost has brought to Jerusalem not only youngsters from the country, each with a handful of coppers to spend, but also an assembly of wealthy and sophisticated merchants, who have come great distances for big business transacted in gold and precious stones. By now, merchants are setting off for home with the tall, sleek, haughty camels they have bought at breath-taking prices, and Arabs astride their beautiful horses are galloping off with heavy saddle-bags.

Reports, however, continue to come in of crowded streets still buzzing with excitement, for today has been a Pentecost with a difference. A select company of more than a hundred men assembled this morning somewhat mysteriously in the Coppersmith's Guildhall in expectation of some dramatic demonstration. Jonathan ben Etchel reports:

(Fade in street noises)

REPORTER   Out of the day's confusions it seems that some strangely convincing dreams, or compelling impulses, or other undeniable signs have been responsible for some one hundred and twenty men, mostly unknown to each other, setting their faces towards Jerusalem for this Pentecost Day, expecting some news or demonstration connected with Jesus of Nazareth.

Last night, in Simeon's Inn, I thought I recognised a particular face. After searching my memory, I went up to a tall man, and said, "Aren't you the Cyrenian who carried Jesus' cross?"

<u>Pentecost</u>

      (Fade out street noises, fade in pub
      background noises)

SIMON CYRENE	(hesitantly) That's right, but who? Of course, Radio Jerusalem!
REPORTER	Then I was mistaken in thinking you were only a visitor in Jerusalem at that time!
SIMON CYRENE	Not at all. I left at daybreak next morning after becoming involved in that soul-sickening tragedy. I vowed never to set foot in Jerusalem again. Never!
REPORTER	But ....
SIMON CYRENE	You see, business was bad - our worst season ever - hardly worth the expense of bringing my caravan. I was half-minded not to do it again. Then that dreadful Friday morning, when I was accidentally entangled in the crucifixion of the young Galilean. The filthy injustice and inhumanity of it, that settled it! I'd <u>had</u> Jerusalem!
	(Pause)
REPORTER	But, so soon, and you <u>are</u> back?
SIMON CYRENE	True, and no one's more surprised than me. We were well on the way home, over the Nile in fact, when I had a particularly odd dream. A young man appeared in it, telling me to send my caravan on, because I must return to Jerusalem for Pentecost. "Not even the Emperor himself could persuade me to return to that place," was my retort. "You may defy Caesar," he replied, "but you will obey my Master. You carried his cross - remember?" "But he's dead - I saw him die," I cried. "Yes, he was dead, but he became alive again - look!" And he held out something at the end of a gold chain from around his neck. Even that small replica of it made me shudder. That's the last thing in the world I should have chosen as an ornament - of all things, a cross!
REPORTER	And was that the end of this encounter?

66

Jerusalem: Herodian masonry flanking tall buildings

SIMON
CYRENE   Eh? Er - no - not quite. He said that this device, the cross, was destined to become the most beautiful and powerful emblem in the world'. I can't explain it - nor my action in sending my caravan on. Well, here I am'.

(Fade out pub noises, fade in street effect)

REPORTER   Others already in the city for the Guildhall meeting included Jairus of Gesara - I understand Jesus healed his daughter - Joseph of Arimethea, and a Centurion from Capernaum. Like the Cyrenean, their accounts of how they had come expectantly to Jerusalem for Pentecost were - well, strange, to say the least. But there was no doubting their sincerity and determination.
This morning, soon after 8 o'clock I was out in the teeming narrow streets of the Lower City. The day was already warm as I made for the meeting at the Copper-smith's Guildhall. On the way I made company with the young Jewish teacher, Saul of Tarsus, who is making quite a name for himself in the few weeks he has been back in Jerusalem.
As we walked and talked neither of us noticed a gathering cloud overhead until a gust of wind swept along the street almost bowling us over. Within seconds the wind was furious enough to make walking almost impossible. After rounding a corner with some difficulty all further progress was blocked by a mass of people filling the street. Buffetted by wind and men and women, I did manage this recording:

(Fade out street noises, fade in jabbering crowd effects and howling wind)

What's happening?

1st BYSTANDER   The Nazarenes have returned to Jerusalem.

REPORTER   Why the excitement?

2nd BYSTANDER   They've been meeting in the upper room of the Guildhall over there. Without warning this wind roared through the street - it seemed to rattle the Guildhall.

1st BYSTANDER   Some say there were flames licking around the folk in that room.

2nd BYSTANDER   And what about that weird speaking in tongues? Fair gives you the creeps!

PHARISEE   They're raving drunk - or they've come back to make trouble.

REPORTER   I see by your fringed robe that you are a Pharisee. What do you really make of all this?

PHARISEE   After the lies about their leader's death, all this non-sense of reappearance. I've seen nothing of him! After that, how could anyone believe them? Drunken rabble!

1st WOMAN   That's right, sir, you tell 'em. Too much new wine! wonder where they get it.

2nd WOMAN   Look - before he was crucified that Nazarene did promise to return, we heard him!

2nd BYSTANDER   And the word's out that he might appear today!

PHARISEE   Well, I have better things to do than wait for a crucified rebel to return from the dead. What next? Let me through please - out of my way there! Are you coming Master Saul?

SAUL   Hold on! Who's that on the balcony?

PHARISEE   Where? Ah! Newly returned to Jerusalem you wouldn't know, Master Saul. That's the Galilean called Simon Peter   (expresses disgust)   the one who denied the Nazarene in the courtyard of the High Priest's palace the night he was arrested. The nerve of the fellow, parading himself publicly!

SIMON PETER   (over crowd noises which gradually subside)   Fellow-Jews and all who are living in Jerusalem, listen, let me explain. These men and I, we are not drunk as some of you suppose. It is, after all, only 9 o'clock in the morning of this great feast day. No, this is something which was predicted by the prophets, for God said of old:

"I will pour out my Spirit on all mankind".
Men of Israel - hear me. Jesus of Nazareth was a man
proved to you by God himself, through miracles and
deeds which were amazing demonstrations of divine
power in action. You saw all this yourselves, and yet -
you killed him, you had him crucified by heathens. Now,
God has brought him back to life again.

    (Crowd murmurings)

Men and brother-Jews, remember the patriarch David.
Just as surely as he himself lived and died, David fore-
saw the resurrection of Christ. He spoke of this, he
spoke of it unmistakably.
Well, that resurrection of Jesus by God is now a fact, a
fact of which we are all eye-witnesses. He has given
this demonstration of the Holy Spirit. _That_ is what you
have seen and heard - that is what you are seeing and
hearing right now.
Brothers, let the whole nation of Israel hear! Beyond
any shadow of doubt, let it be proclaimed that this Jesus,
whom you crucified, God has made both Lord and Christ.

    (Silence, then pandemonium. Fade back to
    street effect)

REPORTER   The ensuing pandemonium made recording impossible.
The strained silence that followed Simon Peter's impassioned declaration was quickly broken by cries of
"What shall we do? What shall we do?" It was taken
up on every side as the crowds surged towards the Guildhall. I lost the young teacher Saul and the Pharisee in
the press of the crowd.
The Guildhall emptied, and the newly commissioned men
(hard to believe that they had ever been afraid, had run
away or cowered in hiding) now radiantly, confident,
they moved out shouting ecstatically, "The Kingdom of
God has come for all who believe in Him!" They
scattered through the city. Soon it seemed that they
were everywhere spreading their good news. Why! I
even saw two of them stop a group of Roman soldiers in

the street to tell their news of the new kingdom: the
soldiers were so stunned by the audacity of it all, they
made no move to detain them!
And so it has gone on throughout the day, and to such
effect that less than twelve hours after this morning's
outburst, the Nazarenes are claiming nearly 3,000 con-
verts. If this is true, they already have the largest
congregation in Jerusalem!
Later, indeed, only an hour ago, the High Priest allowed
me to question him in the Temple precincts - surely
another sign of the unsettling nature of this day's events,
and particularly in the presence of a number of his
colleagues!
I asked him about the massive reaction in support of
the Nazarenes:

>	(Fade out street noises, fade in Temple
>	choir music)

CAIAPHAS	Our people are confused, unhappy, gullible, tormented!
They look for signs from heaven, so charlatans, maniacs,
and misguided simpletons are more than ready to <u>give</u>
them "signs from heaven".

REPORTER	My Lord Caiaphas, is it not possible that these really
could be, as you call them, "signs from heaven"?

CAIAPHAS	Do you not suppose then that I should know of them?

>	(Pause)

And yet - these are hard times. We can almost feel the
marrow rotting in our bones, and the spirit choking in our
throats. All of us need a sign from God. What with
alien soldiers in the streets, sickness round every
corner, and patriots being executed .... What with
doubt and grief and even panic stinking like sewage in
our towns and villages, "Surely", we say, "surely God
has not abandoned us?"

GROUP	(denials) "Master!" "Never let it be said." (etc.)

SINGLE VOICE	(coming right through) God will never abandon us!

CAIAPHAS   True, my friends, very true.

                 (Pause)

REPORTER   It is being suggested My Lord that this might be the
                 moment ....

CAIAPHAS   (cutting in)   The moment when we should be tested by
                 our Lord God.   (pause, then as preaching)
                 When our forefathers fled from Egypt did God abandon
                 them?

GROUP   No! No! No!

SINGLE VOICE   (coming through them)   He parted the waters.

CAIAPHAS   When Jericho stood, stone-walled, in the paths of the
                 promised land, did God abandon Joshua?

GROUP   No! No! No!

SINGLE VOICE   (coming through them)   The walls fell down!

CAIAPHAS   Nor did God abandon us when our people were carried off
                 in captivity to Babylon. Our people sat down by the
                 rivers of Babylon, and they hung their harps on the trees,
                 and they wept when they remembered Zion.
                 And so now too they weep. God did not abandon them in
                 the days of old, and so he will not abandon us now.

GROUP   Amen! Indeed! Truly! Alleluia! Lord be praised!
                 (ad libs)

                 (Fade out choir)

CAIAPHAS   But our God is a jealous God, and He will not be mocked.
                 Not by soldiers, not by tramps or carpenters, and not by
                 men babbling of wind and fire.

                 (Silence)

REPORTER   Thank you Lord Caiaphas.

                 (Fade back to street noises)

                 At certain critical moments in history, young men have
                 seen visions, old men have dreamed dreams. At this

moment, mid-evening of Pentecost in Jerusalem, there are those who declare that nothing like today's events has ever happened in the world before - nothing like it at all!

(Pause)

Now back to the studio.

(Fade out street effects)

NEWSCASTER   The rest of the news:
Yesterday King Harith IV took the salute at a large parade of Nabatean troops in Petra. Inspecting crack units of the Royal Nabatean Camel Corps and the Petra Cavalry Squadron, the King congratulated the troops on their drill and displays of mounted agility. Once again he hinted at some future action, I quote: "to take revenge on the lecherous Tetrarch Herod".
The famous library of the monastery at Qumran, near the Dead Sea, has allowed two more scrolls to go on show for privileged visitors: a very fine scroll of Isaiah the prophet and the Qumran community's own "Manual of Discipline". The Isaiah scroll is 3 metres long when unrolled and contains the prophet's writings set out in 54 parallel columns. It took 17 pieces of leather sewn together to make this scroll. As for the "Manual", we hope to be able to give extracts from this important scroll in future programmes.
From Rome we have a brief report that Lucius Aelius Sejanus has called upon the Senate to intensify its efforts to promote a campaign to "Clean up Roman society".
It is not clear whether Sejanus is really concerned with a clean-up or with the removal of political rivals!
Late news, as usual, at 11 o'clock.
Good evening!

(Station music
and fade out)

Evening News Bulletin VII

THE STONING OF STEPHEN

Newscaster

Sports Reporter, Ian bar Swilon

Roman Centurion

Innkeeper, Levi

Reporter, Jonathan ben Etchel

Simon Peter

Stephen

1st Legionary

2nd Legionary

Jewish Woman, Rhoda

Saul of Tarsus

Crowd

(Fade in station music . . . .)

NEWSCASTER   This is Radio Jerusalem, and waiting for you on the line from Rome we have our sportsman, Ian bar Swilon, with his monthly sports report:

BAR SWILON   And the big talking point here? Who is going to be "Charioteer of the Year"? A few weeks ago the reigning champion, Timon from Carthage, seemed to have it all wrapped up, but a run of brilliant victories by the chief contender for the title has brought Lucius the Macedonian within six points of the champion. With only one month's driving to come, this has all the makings of a grandstand finish to this year's championship.
200,000 fans roared themselves hoarse over Lucius's magnificent comeback after having been badly baulked on

the last lap of Friday's Apennine Cup here in Rome.
Driving his scarlet and bronze chariot with superb skill
he forced his Libyan stallions through an impossible gap
to wrest what seemed certain victory out of the hands of
Theodorus of Tyre in the last 40 yards. This brilliant,
last-minute dash brought him three valuable points in the
championship <u>and</u> the prize of 20,000 sestertii.
But for sheer thrills the third bend on lap 4 of the
Apennine Cup was unforgettable. Five of the chariots
were bunched close as they swung into the turn. The
three inside ones locked together with a tremendous,
sickening crash. Sparks crackled, chariots splintered
apart. Instantly the centre one, the Corinthian, was
crushed to pulp. In the second chariot the Byzantine
was catapulted into the stone boundary wall and broke
his neck. The third driver, the Sidonian, got entangled
in his reins as his chariot disintegrated. He pitched to
the ground, right in the track of Lucius, who had the
wall next behind and couldn't stop or turn. He went full
speed into the wreck, over the Sidonian, into his four,
all mad with fear. What a shambles! Then out of the
turmoil of mangled flesh, fighting horses, resounding
cracks, sand and splinters, out shot Lucius. Next he
took Theodorus, and the race was <u>won</u>!
Once again there was brawling on the terraces, especially between stable boys of rival owners. Four were
killed and eight seriously injured, but the stadium ste-
wards decided not to hold an official enquiry since
little actual damage was done. In my next report, four
weeks today, I'll be able to give you the "Charioteer of
the Year". Till then, from Rome, goodbye.

NEWSCASTER   Thank you, Ian - and what a contest that's building up to.
Death in the Roman arena! Well, <u>that's</u> all in the game,
isn't it?
But death on our Jerusalem streets! That's another matter
altogether, one for grave concern, as Jonathan ben Etchel
has been investigating throughout this, the first day of
the latest Imperial edict:

<u>The Stoning of Stephen</u>

(Scene, a square in Jerusalem, with a noisy
crowd gathered, and sounds of drums
approaching. A centurion and soldiers descend
on the crowd, pushing, beating and kicking
them into silence. The centurion reads from
a scroll)

CENTURION   By Imperial Decree of his majesty the Emperor Caesar
Tiberius it is declared that there shall be no further
assembling of the blasphemers who call themselves
Christians.
There will be no further mention, in public or in private,
of the name of Jesus the Galilean, who was found guilty
of treason, blasphemy, and offences against the peace
of Jerusalem and the Roman Empire, and who was executed for these crimes.
Any persons found consorting in such a fashion as before
mentioned shall be executed immediately and without
trial.
This edict is to be considered the first and last official
warning.

(The centurion barks an order, the detachment
marches off to a drum beat.   Crowd noises
build up again)

INNKEEPER   About time too. We'll have less trouble with these
Christians now.

REPORTER   Ah, Levi the Innkeeper, so the Christians have been
giving you trouble?

INNKEEPER   (defiantly)   It is enough that their sect is in disfavour
with the Government.

REPORTER   That wasn't what I asked you. Have these Christians,
who were being knocked about in the square there only
minutes ago, have they given <u>you</u> cause for complaint?

INNKEEPER   (cagily)   Well, it all depends what you mean by ....

REPORTER   Do they steal, lie, fight? Do they get drunk? Are they
brawlers? Tell me, what sort of people are they?

Jerusalem: outside the old city walls

The Stoning of Stephen

INNKEEPER   If you put it like that, sir . . . .

REPORTER   I do!

INNKEEPER   (reluctantly)   In truth, I cannot complain. They are quiet, honest and truthful.   (Defiantly again)   But the Procurator has decreed against them, and we cannot tolerate blasphemy!

REPORTER   And what would that be exactly? What is it these people blaspheme, Levi?

INNKEEPER   They have no respect for the Temple!

REPORTER   Does that make them peculiar? Does that single them out for persecution?

INNKEEPER   (piously)   The religion of our people must be protected, sir.

REPORTER   Mm . . . .   (innkeeper begins to move off)
Innkeeper - a moment! That waitress of yours there, serving at tables, she's weeping her heart out!

INNKEEPER   Eh? Oh, her! Her father was killed this morning.

REPORTER   Killed! You mean, in one of these crowd clashes with soldiers?

INNKEEPER   That's right.

REPORTER   And you're still making her wait at table?

INNKEEPER   It's her job isn't it? That's what she's paid for. Not my fault her father's been killed!

             (Fade down sound effects. Interruption by two well-favoured men at nearby table)

1st MAN   Sir! Would you take refreshment with us? Like you, we find this Christian business intriguing.

2nd MAN   (obviously continuing earlier conversation)   If this is in fact a hoax - that Jesus bar Joseph of Nazareth did not die on the cross, but was still alive when carried to the tomb and later rescued by his followers - what's the point?

78

<u>The Stoning of Stephen</u>

1st MAN   As the Romans say, "Who gains?" Hardly this Jesus
             fellow. He's disappeared again, you know.

REPORTER   Completely?

1st MAN   Completely! Not a sign or word of him anywhere, so I'm told.

REPORTER   Then what are these Christians up to now?

2nd MAN   You might well ask! It's pathetic really. They don't even
             defend themselves against the Romans. There's no fight
             in them, not like there is in the Essenes and Zealots.

1st MAN   Not as though they were the sort who seek honour or fame
             and fortune. No suggestion even of being prophets.

2nd MAN   Must be mad, the lot of them, to risk prison and torture
             for a mere hoax. No! Even the mad aren't that daft. I
             mean, to invite a public beating and hatred for some-
             thing you know is a lie. Beats me!

1st MAN   What is it that makes them behave like men of the
             deepest conviction, so certain of their faith? Hoax or no
             hoax, it's obvious they do believe.   (Dropping voice)
             And I hear hundreds of folk are catching this belief at
             illegal, late night meetings.

             (Fade out sound effects)

REPORTER   From the square I made my way to the principal meeting
             house of the Christians, the place they call "the
             Ecclesia". This is a large, old building, formerly a
             bazaar, where the Christians, some three hundred or
             more at times, share in common meals. Those who <u>can</u>
             bring food. It is said that some have disposed of their
             property in the country and are living here now - quite a
             colony of them.
             This community is founded on the principle of caring love,
             but rumour has it that there are those among them given
             to dissatisfaction and quarreling. Apparently living
             together in a closed community is no guarantee of
             good will.
             At the house I found a meeting in progress. I slipped

79

inside – remarkably quiet for such a large, mixed gathering. Up front was the impressive figure of the Galilean, Simon, known as the Big Fisherman. He was reading from a tattered scroll.

(Fade in large hall sound effect)

SIMON PETER   The people that walked in darkness have seen a great light. They that dwell in the shadow of death, upon them the light shines. For unto us a child is born. Unto us a son is given. The government shall be upon his shoulder, and . . . .

(CRASH of door flung open. Military commands, clatter of swords on shields, shouts and screams from crowd. Centurion calls "HALT")

CENTURION   You there, are you the one they call the Big Fisherman?

SIMON PETER   (boldly)   I am, and this is a peaceful assembly. You have no right to break it up.

CENTURION   Who are you to talk of rights?

SIMON PETER   Has any one of us committed a crime? If so, take me for trial.

CENTURION   (sharply)   That's what I'm here for, to do just that.

SIMON PETER   On what charge?

CENTURION   Blasphemy and treasonable utterances. Take him away.

(Outcry begins, quelled by Simon Peter)

SIMON PETER   Do not resist.   Be of good cheer. I shall come back to you.

(Sounds of marching boots, stifled cries and screams)

CENTURION   That you will not! Quick March!
The rest of you, if you know what's good for you, get back to your homes. You've seen the last of your Fisherman!

<u>The Stoning of Stephen</u>

(Fade out sound effects)

REPORTER As I walked past the few blocks on the rim of the congested market district, where the shabby hovels of the very poor huddle close to reeking alleys, I encountered much excitement, frantic chatter and gesticulations. The word had gone before me that the Christians' meeting place had been invaded, emptied and locked up. When I overheard that <u>other</u> <u>leaders</u> had been dragged off to prison and that Simon the Fisherman was to be beheaded, I counted myself fortunate to have got away from the place so easily.
Still out and about with my microphone at mid-afternoon, I came across a crowd listening to an impassioned speech. Remembering my narrow escape of the morning, I looked around carefully. A nearby company of Legionaries were leaning negligently on their spears, apparently showing no interest. Mixing with the fringe of the crowd I learned that the speaker was a Greek, Stephen, who had assumed leadership of the Christians on the detention of Simon. He'd been dragged out for questioning, but as I listened it was obvious that he'd taken over the initiative. Without mincing any words, he was appealing to reason and <u>not</u> for mercy. Boldly, yet without defiance, he was making his fearless stand. This was no rabble-rousing speech, but a scathing indictment of Jerusalem's leaders.

(Fade in crowd noises)

STEPHEN You call yourselves the Chosen People! Your ancestors struggled out of one bondage into another, century after century, always looking for a Deliverer, yet <u>never</u> heeding your great teachers when they arose with words of wisdom!
Again and again, inspired leaders have arisen among your people, only to be thwarted and reviled, not so much by the poor and needy - but by the likes of <u>YOU</u>!

(Crowd uproar)

(projecting over noise)   Tell me, which of the prophets

did your fathers <u>not</u> persecute? Now <u>you</u> have become the betrayers, the murderers of the Just One!

(General outcry, shouts of "Blasphemer")

<u>You</u>, <u>you</u>, who claim to have received your law from God himself, how have <u>you</u> kept it?

(Infuriated roar mounts - clatter of microphone falling to ground)

REPORTER   At that point my microphone was dashed from my hand whether deliberately or accidentally in the crush I couldn't say. Stones began to fly. At first only the occasional stone hit its target. The Greek wiped blood from his face. In no time he was shielding his bleeding head with his arms. The stones were coming faster and with telling effect. Believe me, this was no impulsive, impromptu incident. The men throwing stones were mostly expert.
The roar of the crowd was bestial, and all the while the Centurion and his men appeared <u>not</u> to notice what was going on.
Even as the Greek, Stephen, lay dead, or at least un-conscious, there were those who continued to stone him. Then, unbelievably, that broken body was slowly rising on to one elbow. The crowd hushed. The blood-spattered face looked up and the bruised lips broke into a smile. His arm reached out, and his shout, nothing short of triumphant, split the air:
"I see him! I see him! My Lord Jesus, take me!"
The eyes closed, the head dropped, the body crumpled. Stephen was dead - a <u>man stoned to death</u>, out there in the open, on one of our city's streets!
In stunned silence the crowd soon dispersed, many scurrying away, obviously frightened. Straightening up from recovering my microphone from the ground, I found myself looking into the bewildered eyes of a tall legionary. His comrade looked no less disturbed.

(Retreating crowd noises fade into street effect)

<u>The Stoning of Stephen</u>

1st LEGIONARY We should have stopped it.

2nd LEGIONARY How could we? We obey orders, and our orders were not to interfere unless riot threatened.

1st LEGIONARY I still say we should have stopped it.

REPORTER No, your friend is right, you <u>are</u> under orders.

1st LEGIONARY That was a strange thing at the end, sir.

2nd LEGIONARY Probably stranger than you think!

REPORTER What makes you say that?

1st LEGIONARY Well, I'd have sworn the Greek was dead. Then he lifted himself up. Did you see it? He was smiling!

2nd LEGIONARY (thoughtfully) By the look on his face you'd think he saw someone coming to rescue him!

WOMAN (vehemently) He <u>did</u> see someone coming to rescue him!

2nd LEGIONARY (gently) This is no place for a woman unless .... did you know this Greek?

WOMAN He is .... he was my husband-to-be, <u>my</u> Stephen.

REPORTER Tell me, you said he <u>did</u> see someone?

WOMAN Y - e - s.

1st LEGIONARY That dead Galilean maybe?

WOMAN (more lively) That Galilean is not dead, sir. He's more alive than any of us!

2nd LEGIONARY This bloody stoning to death has unnerved her.

WOMAN Stephen is not dead - he went away with Jesus!

REPORTER You really believe that?

WOMAN Jesus may never come for me, Sir! He may never come for you, but he came for Stephen! I saw my Stephen welcomed into Jesus' kingdom. You all saw it, didn't you?

(Fade out street noises)

REPORTER   On my way back to the studio I encountered a bookish-looking young man. I'd seen him earlier - he had been on the fringe of the crowd, and as he held the robes of some of the stone-throwers his face had been contorted with rage. His anger seemed little abated when I questioned him.

(Fade in street noises)

SAUL   (furiously)   The man was a blasphemer! He even had folk believing that he could work "signs and wonders"! Is that likely in such a fanatical young Greek heretic, who has torn our Hebrew history and traditions to pieces? What sort of fellow is it who tells all and sundry that God's truth is for them? Why, he dared to label our great forefathers as "rebels" - rebels who deliberately went against God's plain commands! And as for his wild mouthings about God not needing a place like the Temple - I ask you, what could that young whipper-snapper know of such things? Who did he think he was? Not even a decent Jewish name, and blasting off about our being narrow and hidebound, telling us that our God is too small! It's more than flesh and blood can stand. The man was a dangerous rabble rouser, a blasphemer!

REPORTER   How does blasphemy compare with murder?

SAUL   There's no greater crime than blasphemy!

REPORTER   Of course, I've got it! You're the young teacher who's pulling such crowds. Tell me, as a man of learning, how do <u>you</u> justify this afternoon's brutality?

SAUL   (more calmly)   Come to the Rabbinical School tomorrow, my friend, and I'll enlighten you. Ask for Saul - Saul of Tarsus.

(Fade out street noises)

NEWSCASTER   Now for the rest of the news.
Rumours that Jewish men were to be conscripted for service with the Roman army have now been officially denied. The vast majority of troops in the Jewish provinces are recruited from Syria and are, of course,

non-Jewish. According to Jewish tradition it is not lawful
for a Jew to carry weapons on the Sabbath, nor can he
take part in the religious parades in honour of idols.
Food laws prohibit his eating certain meats. For these
reasons the authorities have agreed to take no further
action to enforce conscription on young Jews.
From the army to the navy, for news of the large pirate
fleet from the North that has terrorised parts of the
Mediterranean for many months. Having rowed down the
Bosporus, sunk galleys galore off Byzantium and
Chalcedon, and swept the Propontis, they burst through
into the Aegean Sea with more destruction and looting. A
Roman squadron of some hundred galleys, commanded by
Tribune Quintus Arrius, was the first to come within
striking distance of the raiders with news that some
eighty pirate galleys had completely destroyed the fleet
stationed in the Thracian Bosporus. Tribune Arrius is
reported to have exercised a pincer movement against
the pirates in the Gulf of Euripas. It succeeded
brilliantly, but not without great loss among the Roman
galleys. The Tribune's own flagship, "Astrea", was
sunk, and the Commander-in-Chief flung into the sea in
full armour. He was saved from certain drowning by a
galley-slave, who is said to be a young Jew from
Jerusalem. Who is this young man? Was his home in
Jerusalem? Of which family?
In our late news at the usual hour of 11 o'clock, we
hope to have more details for you of this young Jew in
the Roman navy, and of his heroism.
Until then,
                    good evening.

                (Station music
                 and fade out)

Evening News Bulletin VIII

THE CONVERSION OF SAUL

Newscaster

Malluch, Phoenician caravan leader

Reporter, Jonathan ben Etchel

Hilell ben Amram, leading Jewish citizen

Maon, Jewish lawyer

Judas, Damascus cobbler

(Fade in station music ....)

NEWSCASTER   This is Radio Jerusalem, and at a time of the year when our city seems more than usually populated with travellers - many from distant parts judging by strange costumes and speech - the old question is being asked again. How <u>do</u> the caravan leaders manage to find their course over great deserts when they travel mostly at night to avoid daytime heat? When much of the time no road is visible across the sands, how do they find their way? Is it instinct, or what? With me in the studio is a caravan leader, Malluch. Tell me, sir, how is this instinct developed?

MALLUCH   Well, there's no magic or sorcery involved in finding one's way across the desert. It's very simple really. The stars guide us.

NEWSCASTER   The stars! and is this some secret shared only by a few of you?

MALLUCH   Not at all. My ancestors were Phoenicians. Long ago the supply of shellfish for extracting the purple dye much favoured by our nobility began to run out near the mouth of the Red Sea. Even then we were sending caravans to cities like Ugarit on the coast of the Great Sea, near

A view of Damascus

where Antioch and Seleucia stand. When it was reported that the same sort of shellfish were to be found on that coast, we moved eastward to the shore of the Great Sea, north of where the people your ancestors called the Philistines settled after they were defeated in the delta country of Egypt.

NEWSCASTER   Are you saying that your people up and moved simply for the sake of some favourite dye?

MALLUCH   No, not entirely. Anyhow, although there was plenty of copper in Cyprus, the supply of tin for making bronze was limited, so our seafarers began to search for it in the west. They found the tin they needed in Tartessus – which you know as Spain – but the voyage was long and some definite guides were needed.

NEWSCASTER   Which they found in the stars?

MALLUCH   Eventually, when someone discovered the particular star which the Greeks now call Phoenikas, after the Phoenicians.

NEWSCASTER   And what's so special about <u>that</u> star?

MALLUCH   It hangs always in the north. It never changes, though others move around it. <u>That</u> is our reliable guide.

NEWSCASTER   But what about when you are travelling south?

MALLUCH   (chuckling) Of course Phoenikas is not our guide then, though it is on the return journey. Going south, again there is a particular star more brilliant than all the others. Once you sight that you can head straight for, say, Bosora. On the other hand, twin stars a little to the left of it will guide you to Gesara, and once in Gesara you don't need the stars because you are on the king's highway leading to Egypt.

NEWSCASTER   Then men like yourself can travel anywhere in the desert by following the stars?

MALLUCH   Certainly if you know which stars to follow. It's all a matter of finding the right star to follow.

NEWSCASTER   Thank you, caravan leader Malluch.
Now if there was one man in our City who seemed to have found his particular star to follow throughout his life, it must have been the teacher, Saul of Tarsus. His public actions left no one in doubt as to what he was about and where he was going, including his departure for Damascus a few weeks ago - in fact, soon after the frightful business of the stoning of the Greek, Stephen. However, some conflicting stories have gone the rounds of Jerusalem this past week as to what happened when Saul reached Damascus. Here is Jonathan ben Etchel, newly returned from Damascus. Jonathan, what is the truth of this matter?

REPORTER   Before leaving Jerusalem two weeks ago I asked one of our leading citizens, Hilell ben Amram, for his impressions of this young Pharisee.

HILELL   Saul of Tarsus - or Gaius Paulus, as he is known in his Roman citizenship - is a Pharisee of Pharisees, a man of high estate. As long as I've known him he has been a profound observer of the Law, a man of strict, even narrow religious convictions, and that in spite of his position among Romans.

REPORTER   How true is the reputation he's gained for himself as arrogant and proud?

HILELL   True enough. He never let anyone forget that he was both a Roman citizen and a Jew of a noble and influential family. I suppose it's his temperament. He's given to strong enthusiasms and dogmatism, and fits of haughtiness were common to him.

REPORTER   Wasn't he making himself very well known as a lawyer too?

HILELL   Yes, he has a very supple tongue, like most lawyers, and he couldn't be shifted once he'd taken a stand. For a young man he was enormously rigid - yet, in his pride, very honest. Certainly in courts of law his forensic genius was greatly feared, and admired.

REPORTER   And still, as you say, a young man! Some of his elders must have resented all this?

HILELL   (chuckling at the thought)   No doubt about that! But above all things he _was_ a devout Jew, hating those who even dared to question the Torah in the slightest detail. And let's not forget, he was very close to the High Priest, Caiaphas himself.

REPORTER   Quite! Were you surprised at his reaction to the stories about the man Jesus of Nazareth?

HILELL   Not really. His outrage over this was true to character. On the other hand, it did seem to me that he took it as something of a personal insult. I can still hear the anger with which he said, "Nothing good ever came out of Nazareth!" And he went on, "When God sends us our Messiah, he will arrive like the lightning, in the company of archangels, with the trumpets of the Lord our God. All will know him. How dare this peasant, this carpenter fellow, be proclaimed the Saviour by the ignorant? Blasphemy, that's what it is!" He was consumed with rage. I'm not likely to forget it!

REPORTER   May I ask, did you share his opinions, and this bitter condemnation?

HILELL   No, and Saul knew this. I like to think I keep something of an open mind in such matters, but not Saul. He despised folk in general, as unlettered fools, as knowing nothing of the true Law. I've known him go so far as to say he would confine them to the outer courts of the Temple. "Their smell and their dull faces," he said, "are an insult to God." Like it or not, Saul never left you in any doubt where he stood.

REPORTER   So, three weeks ago, with the High Priest's commission, Saul went on his lawful duty to Damascus to put down what the Romans call insurrection, but what he denounces as blasphemy. Full of vengeance and fury he rode off in company with fellow-lawyers and soldiers. Last week I was in Damascus for Radio Jerusalem.

<u>The Conversion of Saul</u>

(Fade in market street noises)

REPORTER	I am standing in the Street Called Straight, the major thoroughfare of Damascus. This is the main centre for business affairs - most of the big shops are to hand here, and the taverns. In Simeon's Inn I found lawyer Maon. He had travelled with Saul.

(Change sound effects to inside inn)

MAON	Wouldn't even stop overnight at an inn. Drove himself on, and us too, and for what? What's so special about these Nazarenes anyway? We've so many Jewish sects already, one more isn't going to hurt us. What I say is, if these folk are fools enough to believe that their leader is the Messiah and rose from the dead, let them! So what?
REPORTER	If you feel that way, why did you come with Saul?
MAON	Fed up with Jerusalem, never been to Damascus - famous for its Arabian wines, you know! I planned to enjoy myself in Damascus, even if we didn't arrest a single Nazarene.
REPORTER	I see. But tell me what happened to Saul on the way.
MAON	Who knows?
REPORTER	Well, what did <u>you</u> see?
MAON	We were in sight of Damascus. There was the River Barada, and sensing the river the camels quickened their pace. One of them must have jostled Saul's horse. It screamed and reared up - Saul did well to control it. Suddenly we were all struggling with the horses and camels, milling about on the road. The air was full of curses and cracking whips. (shouts) Landlord, more wine! Good stuff this, worth the journey.
REPORTER	I'm sure it is. Please go on.
MAON	Eh?
REPORTER	You were saying the caravan animals were upset.

91

MAON   Oh that! The next thing we knew was Saul on the road,
            must have fallen from his horse. Strange thing was that
            he was speaking out loud, to no one in particular - just
            looking up and talking.

REPORTER   What was he saying?

MAON   Didn't catch the actual words.

REPORTER   Then what?

MAON   I shook him by the shoulder, told him to snap out of it.
            He muttered something about "the heat, must have
            fainted". I asked him if he was fit enough to go on. You
            know what he said?

REPORTER   I've no idea.

MAON   "If you will lead me - I'm blind."
            As sure as I'm sitting here, those were his very words -
            and he was.

REPORTER   Was what?

MAON   Blind! His eyes looked normal enough, but something
            had blinded him.

REPORTER   It all sounds rather weird.

MAON   You can say that again, and that wasn't the end of it by
            half.

REPORTER   How do you mean?

MAON   Our instructions from Caiaphas were to report to Arza,
            ruler of Damascus's largest synagogue, but as we came
            along the main street here, Saul stopped, ordered me to
            take him into a cobbler's shop.

REPORTER   But you said he was blind. How could he . . . .

MAON   (interrupting) How could he know there was a cobbler's
            shop right there? He said he recognised the smell of
            leather. And before I could say a word, there's the
            cobbler himself taking Saul by the arm and welcoming
            him to Damascus!

The Conversion of Saul

REPORTER   The cobbler <u>knew</u> Saul?

MAON   Apparently - seemed to be expecting him. Of course
            that roused my suspicions. I saw it all. Someone in the
            caravan must have given Saul a drug to blind him. Now
            they planned to kill him so that there would be no per-
            secution of the Nazarenes.

REPORTER   What did Saul say to that?

MAON   He laughed at me. Me, Maon, the lawyer - laughed at!
            He dismissed me, there and then. Who does he think he
            is, that's what I'd like to know?

REPORTER   But he hasn't been killed, has he?

MAON   No? Well, it's the devil's work, I say. That's it, a
            devil took possession of him out there on the road.

            (Fade out inn sounds. Fade in cobbler's shop
            effects with market street in background)

REPORTER   It was over the rough stones of this road that Saul of
            Tarsus stumbled after some blinding experience outside
            the City last week. Sightless, what did his other senses
            tell him? The hum of spindle and the slap-slap of loom
            as the shuttle's thrown back and forth, the enticing
            aroma of bread fresh from the oven, the taint of the glass-
            blower's burning sulphur, the tinkle of the silversmith's
            tiny hammer on an anvil, the musty smell of the scribe's
            parchments, the acrid odour of leather; and it was the
            last that attracted Saul.
            I am standing in that same cobbler's shop, with Judas,
            the cobbler:
            Judas, you are a Nazarene. Did you know who the blind
            man was you took into your home the other day?

JUDAS   Yes. I saw Saul of Tarsus once in Jerusalem. I recog-
            nised him out there on the street, and I could tell by the
            way he walked that he was blind.

REPORTER   But this man above all others is your enemy.

JUDAS   Was!

REPORTER   Was? You mean he's not your enemy any more?

JUDAS   That's right.

REPORTER   When you saw him on the street, did you know then that
             he was no longer your enemy?

JUDAS   No.

REPORTER   Didn't you hate him for all the trouble he caused your
             fellow-Nazarenes in Jerusalem?

JUDAS   Someone asked the Master once what was the greatest
             commandment. (quietly) Jesus answered,
             "You shall love the Lord your God with all your heart and
             with all your soul and with all your mind. This is the
             first and great commandment. And the second is similar.
             You shall love your neighbour as yourself. On these two
             commandments hang all the Law and the Prophets."
             No matter what he had done in the past, Saul is my
             neighbour. I could do no less than the Lord commanded.

REPORTER   Your Lord commanded? Are you saying you had a specific
             command about Saul?

JUDAS   Yes. A voice spoke within my soul and commanded me
             to take him in.

REPORTER   Did others hear it?

JUDAS   Jesus spoke to us in his own voice, when he was here on
             earth. Now that he is risen, he speaks only in our souls.

REPORTER   I see!

JUDAS   (with a chuckle)   I don't think you do! Saul heard him
             on the road.

REPORTER   What? Are you saying that's what caused all the rumpus
             in the caravan and struck him blind?

JUDAS   Saul said so. He told me that it was some blinding light
             that started it all. Then there was a voice, a voice he'd
             never heard before but he was in no doubt as to who it
             was speaking to him.

"Saul! Saul!" The tone was gently reproving, he said,
"Why do you persecute me?"
When Saul asked, "Who are you Lord?" he answered, "I
am Jesus whom you persecute. It is hard for you to kick
against the pricks."

REPORTER   The pricks - what does that mean?

JUDAS   Jesus must have called him sometime ago, but he kicked
                against it then, as an ox kicks against the pricks intended
                to drive it on. Now the Master had to strike him blind,
                so that he could no longer resist.

REPORTER   And Saul accepted all this?

JUDAS   Gladly.

REPORTER   I understand he has left you. What was his condition
                when he left? Where is he now, and what is he doing?

JUDAS   So many questions? After a few days Ananias came to
                heal him.

REPORTER   A physician?

JUDAS   Ananias is a weaver.

REPORTER   Then how?

JUDAS   He said the voice of the Lord had instructed him to come
                to Saul and heal his blindness. Gently he touched Saul's
                eyes and said quietly, "Brother Saul, the Lord Jesus who
                appeared to you, has sent me in order that you might
                regain your sight and be filled with the Holy Spirit."
                Immediately Saul shouted, "I see! I see!" In front of
                him there was a bowl of fruit. He seized a pomegranate,
                bit into it, letting the juice stream down his chin. When
                my wife handed him a cup of wine, he drank it thirstily.
                "My friend Maon was right," he exclaimed, "the best
                wine in the world does come from your vineyards, and
                the best pomegranates."

REPORTER   What did he do then?

JUDAS   That's the very question _he_ asked, "What shall I do now?"

<u>The Conversion of Saul</u>

Neither Ananias nor I had the answer to that one. But he
went on. "I shall testify about what has happened to me.
I shall tell the world how Jesus spoke to me on the road
to Damascus, and called me to serve him." He left
Damascus last night.

     (Fade out sound effects)

REPORTER   Barely two weeks ago this man's name was on everyone's
lips here in Jerusalem - by the Jews, hailed and honoured
as teacher and lawyer, destined for greatness: by the
Nazarenes, hated and feared for his fierce denunciation
and destruction. Today, wherever he is, fellow-Jews
reject him, Nazarenes suspect him. Who would be in his
shoes now, when he so vehemently accepts that which
only yesterday he condemned with contempt and loathing?
A Jewish noble and a Roman citizen, a man of proved
intelligence and ingenuity, enthusiastic and adored,
<u>this is certain</u> - we have not heard the last of Saul of
Tarsus.

NEWSCASTER   Thank you, Jonathan ben Etchel. And that's all until the
late news at 11 o'clock.
Until then,
           good evening!

     (Station music
     and fade out)